INSURANCE LEA

CH00724266

RISK MANAGEM...

by

NEIL CROCKFORD

LONDON

WITHERBY & CO. LTD.

32-36 Aylesbury Street

London EC1R 0ET

Tel No. 071-251 5341

Fax No. 071-251 1296

1st Edition 1991

©

WITHERBY & CO. LTD.

1991

ISBN 1 85609 024 8

INTRODUCTION

The " Insurance Learners" Series was first published by Lesley and Page Services Limited over 10 years ago. Some titles are now in their fourth or fifth edition. Learners are aimed at all readers who wish to have a basic grounding in the various aspects of insurance covered by each title. In particular they are invaluable, low cost introductory and revision texts for the qualifying examinations of the: —

Chartered Insurance Institute (CII)
and BTEC

They are also useful additional reading on insurance aspects of other professional examinations and further and higher education courses, and are used extensively within the training departments of insurance organisations.

Most of the Learners include examples of past examination questions and examiners' comments from the Chartered Insurance Institute.

With the introduction of the new CII examination syllabus in 1992, some titles in the series are being extensively revised. For these titles past examination questions are not included, although they will be in future editions. Students using the 'Learners' to help with their examinations should check the current syllabus carefully and revise those parts from the 'Learner' which are most relevant. For CII students, the current Publishers, Witherby & Company Ltd have an up to date list of which titles are most useful for each of the CII examination subjects.

The Learners are not a substitute for the full recommended texts of the examining body concerned, especially the CII. Neither are they an examination "crammer". Rather, they are designed to be used as introductory reading, to get an overview of the subject. Also most importantly, they are an invaluable revision aid, providing a succinct summary of each topic area covered in order to fix the subject in the mind and refresh the memory.

As always, the Publishers and the Authors welcome any comments from readers and would like to thank those who have, in the past, made useful suggestions incorporated in current editions.

655 – RISK MANAGEMENT

KNOWLEDGE BASE

1. The Nature of Risk Management

- The principles and process of risk management.
- The nature of industrial management and organisation and the different styles.
- The place of risk management in the organisational structure.
- The role and methods of operation of the risk manager within an organisation.

2. Risk Analysis

- The techniques of risk identification and measurement including
  - determining the most appropriate method,
  - sources of information.
- The principles and different systems of quality management.
- An outline knowledge of fire protection and security systems.

3. Control and Transfer of Risk

- The techniques of loss control (passive, active and post loss).
- The methods of production and distribution of risk control guidelines.
- The different ways of dealing with risk by means of
  - determining the most effective means of physical risk control,
  - risk transfer,
  - risk financing, including insurance,
  - determining optimum risk retention levels,
  - risk funding,
  - structuring a captive insurance operation.
- The techniques for monitoring and updating risk management programmes.
- The methods of structuring an insurance and risk management manual.
- The methods of structuring an insurance programme (including international programmes).
- The structure of insurance markets in the principal industrialised nations and the ways in which they are regulated including
  - the nature and types of reinsurance structures.

4. Financial Considerations

- Basic accounting principles and the treatment of losses and recoveries for accounting and tax purposes.
- The different methods of cost/benefit analysis (including DCF and NPV calculation) and methods of allocating financial resources.
- The ways of justifying risk management expenditure.

Note to candidates

Candidates will be required to:

- produce risk management solutions for given problems including innovative alternatives;
- create an insurance structure for a specific risk profile;
- create a model risk management policy, strategy and organisation;
- select the most appropriate means and combination of techniques for handling risks.

CONTENTS

CHAPTER 1

INTRODUCTION AND DEFINITIONS

1.01   Two things need to be borne in mind at all times when studying this course and when taking the examinations:

(i)   Risk management is a **practical** subject.

The theory of risk management is very simple and can be learned very quickly. The complexity of the subject, and what the examiners will seek to test, lies in applying the theory to practical problems encountered by industry and commerce. You must therefore always be prepared to support your answers with examples drawn from the trade or industry mentioned in the question, or, if the question is a general one, from an industry you know about.

The examiners do not expect students to be experts about every industry but you should be aware of the major risks facing construction, engineering, chemical, pharmaceutical, oil and transport firms, and those in other important industries. This is not so daunting as it sounds, as these risks are usually obvious and identifying them, like so much else in the study of risk management, is largely a matter of common sense. Nevertheless, the student will find it helps enormously to take any opportunity that presents itself to visit industrial premises and to use the visit to look at them with a risk management eye. If, in answering an examination question, you find it difficult to think of a good industrial example, the risk problems of a large department store or supermarket may often provide a suitable instance.

(ii)   Risk management is a **management** subject, not an insurance one.

Insurance plays a very important part in risk management, but it is not the only solution to be thought of, nor, in most cases, the first one. Students must therefore beware of treating risk management questions with an insurance-biased approach.

Always begin by analysing the nature and causes of the problem. Risk management is as much about using the results of such an analysis to eliminate or reduce the risk, as about finding means of transferring the cost of its effects by insurance.

1.02   **RISK**

'Risk' is a difficult word to define because it is used in so many different ways. To someone in insurance, for example, the same word can mean the thing insured, the peril that threatens it, and the chance of a loss happening.

1

In general, however, there are two main constituents in any definition of risk:

① — **uncertainty** and

② — **undesired consequences**

To these, we can add a third factor:

③ — the need for some **change in existing circumstances** if the risk is to produce its effect. This is important, because while risk itself is often unmanageable, because it is wholly outside our control, it is the fact that something must change before disaster occurs that makes risk management possible, because we can influence the factors that must change. If, for example, a building is at risk from earthquake, the risk will have no effect on it unless its present stability is impaired. We can do nothing to control the risk of an earthquake occurring, but by strengthening the building appropriately, we can control the extent of damage by earthquake.

1.03 ACADEMIC DEFINITIONS OF RISK

The following academic definitions of risk should be noted:

(i) **Risk is potential variation from expected outcomes.**

This implies that the greater the amount by which the outcome of an event may vary, the riskier that event is.

The problem with using this definition for practical purposes is that it makes no distinction between positive and negative outcomes. Thus by this definition an event where the possible range of outcomes in financial term was − £1,000 to + £100,000 would be 'riskier' than one with possible outcomes ranging from − £10,000 to − £5000. This conflicts with the practical view of risk, which would be unlikely to support the view that an event which almost guaranteed a profit was somehow riskier than one which promised a certain loss.

The shortcomings of this definition of risk can be overcome by applying the well-known business concept of **downside risk**, which considers only the potential variation **below a pre-determined minimum acceptable outcome**.

(ii) **Risk is the chance (or probability) of loss.**

By this definition, the greater the probability of loss, the greater the risk.

This definition is open to the following objections:

— as the probability of loss increases, the **uncertainty** diminishes, and the risk becomes more predictable, and therefore more manageable.

2

- it takes no account of the potential severity of loss, which affects one's view on whether or not a risk is acceptable. Many people, for example, would be happy to accept a risk of high probability if only a few pence were at stake, but would find an event of the same probability much too risky if they stood to lose many thousand pounds.

- it ignores the other subjective factors which come into play in deciding what constitutes an acceptable risk. (*see below*)

(iii) **Risk is the possibility that positive expectations of a goal-oriented system will not be realised.**

This definition, proposed by Dr. M. Haller, is a useful one for risk management purposes, because:

- it concentrates on undesired consequences. Like most people in practice, it does not concern itself with the 'risk' that things may go better than expected.

- it accepts that 'positive expectations' may not be expressed in monetary terms. Uninterrupted operation or continued provision of a useful service are positive expectations in themselves.

- it applies to every 'goal-oriented system', whether that system is an individual, a department, a company, a group of companies, a state or the world itself.

1.04 SUBJECTIVE RISK AND ACCEPTABLE RISK

Subjective risk is the extent to which a person feels threatened by a particular risk. This may bear no relation to the objectively-assessed probability of its occurrence. It will be affected by:

- Potential severity of the consequences.

- The extent of the person's knowledge of the risk.

  No-one feels threatened by a risk they have never heard about. A risk may, however, seem much more frightening to someone with a limited amount of information about it than it does to an expert in the subject.

- Familiarity with the risk. Risks which are part of one's everyday life may be treated as being less serious simply because they are familiar. At the same time the threat from a less familiar risk may be perceived as much greater than it really is.

- Psychological factors which mean that some kinds of risk hold greater terrors than others.

- The degree of risk aversion.

  Each person has an individual level of **risk aversion** or **risk preference**. A risk averse person prefers to avoid risk, and looks for security and protection. A risk preferrer is more of a gambler, and is prepared to take more risks. The level of risk aversion or risk preference is not a fixed characteristic — it may vary in the same individual at different ages, or in different circumstances.

— whether the risk is assumed voluntarily. People commonly accept risks in leisure pursuits which they would find unacceptable as part of their working conditions.

Acceptable risk is the level of subjective risk which an individual or organisation feels comfortable in facing.

1.05 PURE AND SPECULATIVE RISKS

Pure risks are those which present the possibility of a loss, but not of a profit. The risks that can be insured against are pure risks, but by no means all pure risks are insurable.

Speculative risks may produce a profit or a loss. Most business risks which are deliberately entered into fall into this category.

The basic principles of managing both types of risk are essentially the same, but the techniques of pure risk management and of the management of financial and other speculative risks have developed separately. This reflects the fact that most firms find it operationally convenient for the management of each type of risk to be handled by different departments.

This course concentrates upon the management of pure risks, but it should be noted that the boundary between the two types of risks is by no means always clear-cut, particularly in such fields as that of political risk.

1.06 STATIC AND DYNAMIC RISKS

Static risks are those which are always present in any society. The risks of fire and of other natural perils are examples of this type of risk. Risks of this kind are usually pure risks.

Dynamic risks are those which change as society changes. Economic, political, social, legal, technological and environmental changes may all create new risks or modify existing ones. Dynamic risks are usually speculative risks, but they include one significant class of pure risks : the risks of liability, which depend entirely upon the development of the law.

1.07 FUNDAMENTAL AND PARTICULAR RISKS

Fundamental risks are those which affect the whole, or a significant part of society, such as major natural disasters or wide-ranging political or economic factors, such as wars or recessions. The individual firm normally has little control over the causes of such risks, and management of them will thus have to concentrate on reducing their effects.

Particular risks are those which mainly affect an individual or a single firm, which may be able to control them to some extent, making a wider range of risk management options possible.

1.08 RISK MANAGEMENT

There is no single universally-agreed definition of risk management. It can be described in very general terms as 'the application of the principles of management decision-making to the particular problems of risk', or as 'the minimisation of the overall cost of risk', but the most useful definition is likely to be one which indicates the processes of risk management, such as:

'the identification, measurement, control and financing of risks which threaten the existence, the assets, the earnings or the personnel of an organisation, or the services it provides'.

CHAPTER 2

THE THEORY OF RISK MANAGEMENT

2.01 MANAGEMENT DECISIONS

The standard method of solving any management problem consists of the following steps:

— identification of the problem;

— evaluation of its potential effects;

— identification and analysis of possible solutions;

— adoption of the most appropriate solution;

— monitoring the results.

2.02 THE STAGES OF RISK MANAGEMENT

Risk management uses this procedure, but special names are given to each of the stages, as follows:

2.03 — **Risk Identification.** Until a risk has been identified as a threat to the individual organisation, nothing can be done to manage it.

2.04 — **Risk measurement.** Measurement of the risk is essential in order to decide the appropriate method of dealing with the risk. It will be of two kinds:

— the measurement of **severity** to determine the maximum effect the risk could have upon the organisation. This measurement should be in financial terms.

— the measurement of **probability** to determine how likely the risk is to produce these adverse effects. This will be expressed as a figure on the scale of probabilities, which ranges from 0 for an event which cannot possibly occur to 1 for an event which is certain to occur.

The processes of risk identification and risk measurement together are sometimes known as **risk analysis**.

2.05 RISK TREATMENT

This stage includes the choice and implementation of the most suitable risk handling procedure. The following methods may be used:

2.06   **Risk avoidance**. A risk can be avoided by abandoning the activity which gives rise to the risk, or by carrying it out elsewhere, by another method or using different materials.

2.07   **Risk reduction**. Action can be taken to reduce the probability of the risk producing its effects or the severity of the loss. While it is not often possible to eliminate the risk completely, risk reduction (or **loss control** as it is also known) can frequently diminish it to a level where it becomes an acceptable risk.

2.08   **Risk transfer**. It may be possible to transfer the risk or its financial consequences to someone else. There are two main methods of transfer:

    — **transfer by contract**. The risk may be transferred by contracting the activity out, or the cost of the loss may be passed on by an exclusion clause in a contract, a limitation of liability, an indemnity or hold harmless agreement or the like.

    — **transfer by insurance**. This very common method of risk treatment passes the financial consequences of the risk to an insurer in return for the payment of a premium.

2.09   **Risk retention**. If the risk is an acceptable one, it may be retained, and the cost of any losses met by the organisation itself. It is often possible for a large organisation to retain more of its risks by pooling similar risks faced by its constituent units and taking advantage of **combination**. While the risks pooled might be too great for an individual unit to bear, the **spread of risk** over the organisation as a whole is sufficient to make the risk suitable for retention.

2.10   **Risk financing** arrangements must be made to cover the cost of retained losses.

    — The smallest losses may be met out of **operating budgets** without special provision.

    — More serious losses may need some form of **loss reserve**, either in the form of an internal **contingency fund** or provided by the establishment of a **captive insurance company**.

    — External financing may be arranged by **borrowing**. The credit market may be approached as necessary after a loss, or it may be possible to arrange a **contingent line of credit** in advance, which can be drawn upon as necessary after a serious loss.

2.11   Other methods of risk treatment have been devised, which are mainly used in the field of financial and other speculative risk, and as such are outside the scope of this course. These include **forward buying, hedging** transactions, **interest rate swaps** and similar arrangements.

2.12   The final stage in the risk management process is to **monitor** the effect of the whole risk management programme, to check that the action taken has been appropriate and to determine whether any changes are necessary. The activities of an organisation, the physical, social and legal environment in which it exists are all constantly changing, and so is the organisation's **risk pattern**. Each of these changing factors may call for a change in the risk management programme.

2.13   THE RISK MANAGEMENT CYCLE

The stages of risk management outlined above are often spoken of, for the sake of convenience, as if they were a serial process, in which each stage is complete before the next begins. This is an oversimplification, and the process in fact consists of a loop. First a risk is identified and then measured in order to see whether its worst effects would be too severe for the organisation to stand. If so, the next stage is normally to attempt risk avoidance or loss control to reduce the risk to an acceptable level.

It must then be re-measured to see whether the objective has been achieved. If not, then further risk reduction measures must be applied and the residual risk measured once again.

This process is repeated until no further reduction is possible, when the risk is transferred or retained according to its size.

The effects of the programme must then be monitored and this in turn leads to further risk identification, because not only will changes within and outside the organisation have affected the risks, but any action taken to manage risk itself inevitably affects the risk pattern. The loop thus begins again, making risk management a never-ending process.

2.14   PROVISIONAL RISK MANAGEMENT DECISIONS

It would clearly be unwise for any organisation to delay all risk management activity until the risks had been thoroughly analysed. The stages of risk management listed above may therefore not be strictly followed, because prudence may, for example, require some risks to be transferred by insurance initially, to provide protection while the successive steps of risk management are carried out.

2.15   THE COST OF RISK

One of the aims of risk management is to reduce the cost of risk to its economic minimum.

The **total cost of risk** is made up of:

9

① — the cost of the existence of risk. Risks may cause companies and individuals to modify their actions. A venture may be abandoned or not undertaken because of the risks involved. There will be an opportunity cost because avoiding the risk means forgoing the potential profit from the activity. There will also be a cost in that customers may have to do without goods or a service which they would prefer to have.

② — the cost of loss prevention or loss reduction.

③ — the cost of transferring risk. This may be in the form of insurance premiums or the risk element in the price for contracting an activity out.

④ — the cost of losses caused by risks which have been retained.

⑤ — the cost of the risk management process itself. The activities of risk identification, measurement and treatment and of monitoring performance all involve administrative and other costs.

2.16 DIRECT AND INDIRECT COSTS

Some of these costs will be **direct costs**. The following are examples of this type of cost:

① — the cost of protective devices and equipment;

② — insurance premiums;

③ — cost of repairing damage, replacing lost property and

④ — compensating those injured where the risk involved has been retained;

⑤ — the salaries of risk management personnel.

The total cost of risk will also include many **indirect costs**, which may be very difficult to quantify. Examples include:

① — effect on production of implementing risk management measures;

② — cost of investigating, reporting and accounting for a loss;

③ — effect on production of a loss — even if production is not interrupted, extra safety precautions may have to be taken, employees' attitudes to work may be affected;

④ — effect on plans for the development of the company — a loss may mean plans must be delayed, changed or abandoned;

⑤ — effect on the public image of the company of a major loss;

⑥ — inconvenience to the public caused by withdrawal of a popular product, either as the result of a defect discovered, or as a safety measure because of possible harmful effects or because of extortion threats involving product contamination.

2.17 PRIVATE AND SOCIAL COSTS

Only some of these direct and indirect costs will have to be met by the organisation that is faced with the risk. Those that fall on it alone are called **private costs**.

Other costs have to be met by society as a whole or some section of the public. These are known as **social costs**.

The fact that some of the costs and effects of risk have to be borne by people who may have no connection with the organisation threatened by the risk, and no prospect of participating in any profit that may be made by accepting it, emphasises the social importance of sound risk management.

CHAPTER 3

RISK IDENTIFICATION

3.01 STAGES IN RISK IDENTIFICATION

Before a risk can be managed in any way, it must be identified. The process of risk identification consists of two stages. The first of these, which may be called **risk perception**, consists of becoming aware of the possibility that a particular type of risk might threaten the organisation.

The second stage, **risk identification proper**, consists of deciding:

- whether such a risk presents an actual threat, and if so, how it might be caused;
- what perils would be involved;
- what the likely consequences would be;
- what characteristics of the organisation increase or decrease the probability of the risk producing its effects or the probable severity of those effects.

3.02 PRINCIPLES OF RISK IDENTIFICATION

The range of potential risks which may threaten an organisation is so broad that **systematic identification** is essential. If a haphazard method or no method at all is used, there will almost certainly be gaps in the identification which could prove disastrous. The following are some of the pitfalls of such an approach:

- Familiar risks may be studied in depth while no imagination is used to identify unusual risks;
- On the other hand, familiar risks may be overlooked because of their very familiarity;
- Experts identifying risks may concentrate on the risks which relate to or which can be countered by their particular form of expertise. Their participation may be essential, especially where complex industrial processes are involved, but an intelligent layman should also be involved in the work of identification so that simple and obvious risks are not overlooked.
- Only those risks which fit existing solutions may be identified. An organisation that sees insurance as its main means of solving risk problems may thus concentrate exclusively upon insurable risks.

Risk identification therefore needs to be planned carefully, using a disciplined approach which will minimise the chances of a potentially catastrophic risk being overlooked.

13

3.03 SOURCES OF INFORMATION

Information for risk identification can be obtained in two ways:

— through **desk research** i.e. by the study of documents, plans and other information produced by the organisation itself, by competitors, trade associations, government departments and others.

— through **site visits**, which give an opportunity to see the areas which may be affected by risk, and to discuss potential risks with those most immediately affected by them.

Both methods are important and they complement each other, thus reducing the chance of failing to identify a serious risk.

3.04 DESK RESEARCH

Available documents may give a good picture of an organisation, which can suggest the types of risk it will be faced with. Important information can be obtained from:

① — annual report and accounts

— can show types of activity, geographical spread of the organisation, main sources of profit, areas of potential development etc.

② — management accounts

— more detailed — many potential threats to the organisation can be identified from the information contained in them about buildings, plant, stock and other resources, the cost of past losses, the organisation's financial situation and arrangements, the dependency of the organisation upon particular suppliers or customers, or of one part of the organisation upon another.

③ — fixed asset registers

— provide information about the type, age and value of plant and equipment. This can indicate:

— processes used and their risks;

— possibility of increased unreliability and obsolescence of older equipment;

— risks of interruption if equipment is difficult to replace e.g. because it is non-standard, obsolete or manufactured abroad.

④ — site plans, photographs and descriptive material about premises

— provide information about layout, operations and surroundings, all of which may have risk implications.

(5) — promotional literature about the organisation

    — information about the organisation's products, aims and the image it seeks to promote with the public.

(6) — manuals of procedure

    — detailed information about particular aspects of the operations, safety and emergency procedures to counter risks already identified by the organisation.

(7) — trade journals, industry and competitor's literature

    — indicates risks common to the industry in which the organisation operates.

(8) — standard trading conditions, contracts, leases and other legal documents

    — can indicate potential liability, credit and other risks.

(9) — safety publications

    — indicate particular risks of the industry and of processes, machinery and materials used.

(10) — insurance records

    — information on risks which have caused loss in the past, and on those covered by (and excluded from) insurance policies.

To make use of the information obtained and obtain a usable picture of the risk pattern of the organisation, the risk identification process must be an ordered one, using one or more of a number of possible techniques.

3.05   CHARTING RISK

No organisation has to start entirely from scratch in identifying risk. There will always be some information about:

— accidents and losses which have already occurred;

— the common hazards of the trade or the processes and materials used;

— the risks loss prevention devices already installed are designed to counter;

— the assets and the people the organisation wishes to safeguard;

— disastrous occurrences the organisation wishes to avoid.

This information can be used as the starting point for risk identification by setting it out in tabular form.

A four column table may be used, with the headings:

Threats	Resources	Consequences	Modifying Factors

3.06 THREATS

In this column are listed all the perils which threaten the organisation. Initially, these may be listed in broad terms such as fire, storm, earthquake, liability, machinery breakdown, gradual deterioration etc. Later in the identification process, these perils may be much more closely defined.

3.07 RESOURCES

In this column are listed all the building, equipment, materials, personnel, suppliers, customers and others on whom the organisation relies for its continued existence and prosperity.

3.08 CONSEQUENCES

In this column are listed the undesirable effects of perils acting the resources of the organisation. It might thus include such things as interruption of production, need to withdraw or recall a product, death or injury of employees or others etc.

3.09 MODIFYING FACTORS

This column will record the particular features which affect the impact the occurrence of listed threats would have upon the listed resources. Presence or absence of loss prevention devices, standby equipment, alternative sources of supply, proximity to a river with a history of flooding, etc. might all be entered here.

3.10 USING THE CHART

Known risk features can be entered in the appropriate column of the chart and further items added as they are identified. The advantage of the chart is that an entry in one column may enable further entries to be made in other columns. Thus one item in the list of resources may suggest a threat which could affect that particular asset which had been omitted from the list of threats, but which might be important in other areas. The list of consequences to be avoided may suggest threats which would bring a particular loss about, or resources which would have to be affected for that loss to occur. Modifying factors may themselves suggest new risks. Sprinklers, for example, may reduce the fire risk, but create a new risk for materials sensitive to water damage or to changes of humidity.

The charting method can be used in general terms to identify the risks of the organisation as a whole, or in a much more detailed form to identify, for example, the risks to a single key piece of equipment.

3.11 CHECKLISTS

The basic risk identification tool is the **checklist**, which serves the primary purpose of triggering the imagination of the person using it. No checklist can ever be complete and the points in it should be thought of only as starting points for thought.

Checklists may be constructed on the basis of:

— threats;

— resources;

— undesired consequences;

They may start out as standard lists designed to be used by any organisation, as an adaptation of some record (such as a plant register) already in existence, or as a list drawn up by the risk manager from first principles. Inevitably, they will have to be modified in use to meet the needs of the individual organisation. The chief disadvantage of the checklist is that, however full it is, there will always be gaps in it, and these gaps may mean that important risks are not identified. This danger can be reduced, although not eliminated entirely, by using two or more checklists using different starting points.

3.12   EVENT ANALYSIS

This technique uses as its starting point a particular loss-producing event, such as a fire, a major theft, or a defective batch of products. When such an event has been identified, its causes and consequences are analysed, in order to identify ways in which the organisation could be faced with such a loss, and what the effects would be, both in financial terms and in the creation of further risks. As the analysis proceeds in each direction it becomes less general and more specific. The use of **hazard logic trees**, by which the causes of the loss are tabulated, and then the possible causes of those causes, and so on until all the sources of loss are revealed is particularly useful in the analysis. The procedure is shown in the following diagram:

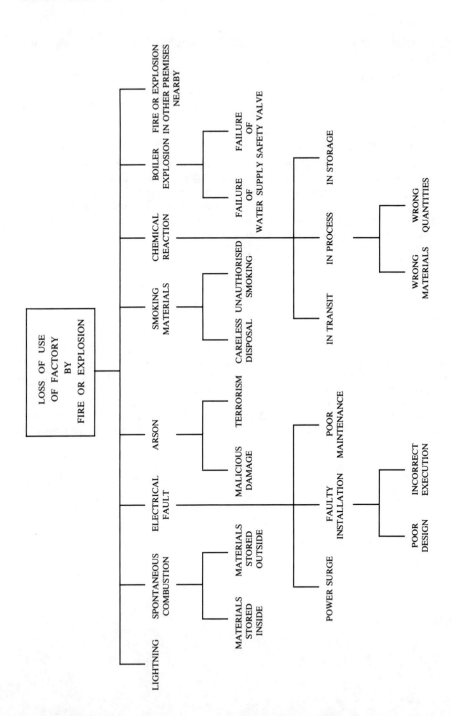

Fig. 1 : Hazard Logic Tree

3.13 FAULT TREE ANALYSIS

This is an alternative method of tracing potential sources of loss and thus of giving information about risk. Starting once again from a specific loss-producing event, this technique sets out the conditions that are necessary, either individually or in combination, to bring the event about. The same logic is applied to each of the conditions so identified, and the procedure is repeated as many times as necessary. A typical analysis of this kind is shown below. The merit of this technique is that it highlights situations which may present no risk on themselves, but which could endanger the organisation if they were to exist together.

3.14 HAZARD AND OPERABILITY STUDIES (HAZOPs)

This technique was designed by ICI for use at the planning stage of process plants in order to identify and eliminate potential causes of failure. It can be adapted, however, to any kind of operation or organisational system and its principles used to identify risks of all kinds. It consists of the posing of the repeated question, "What would happen if ..." at every stage of the operation, guided by a set of simple keywords such as:

- NO
- MORE
- LESS
- AS WELL AS
- PART OF
- REVERSE
- OTHER THAN

Using the keyword NO, for example, one would consider the consequences of the absence of any variable — pressure, temperature, concentration and so on at each stage of the process, and how such a situation could come about. A similar examination would be carried out using each of the other keywords, to give a full analysis of the risks inherent in the system. If the analysis is carried out at the design or planning stage, it should then be possible to redesign the operations so as to eliminate the risks revealed or reduce them to manageable proportions.

3.15 THE DOW INDEX

This is an example of a risk identification and quantification system designed to meet the special needs of a particular industry. It was designed by Dow Chemical Company to identify the particular fire and explosion risks in chemical plants and storage installations, and consists of the following steps:

(i) to list all materials, by products and catalysts present in the operation;

(ii) to identify the dominant substance in terms of quantity and hazard presented;

   (iii) to quantify the hazards present according to their potential for combustion, decomposition or reaction;

   (iv) to apply special rating factors from the Dow Fire and Explosion Guide (based on a study of many accidents and hazardous situations in the past) to allow for quantities of materials or the type of process involved.

3.16 SAFETY AUDITS

This is an example of risk management taking advantage of a technique originally designed for the identification of one particular type of risk. Like the financial audit from which it derives its name, a safety audit is an examination of the way to check:

   (i)   That there is an adequate awareness of possible risks;

   (ii)   That a system exists to minimise them;

   (iii) That the system is observed and is working well.

This process will, in the nature of things, reveal risks which have not been catered for, and it is therefore a useful method of risk identification.

3.17   The audit, whether concerned with its original purpose of examination if a company's safety performance, or in its extended version of a full risk management investigation is carried out by a group of qualified people from different disciplines, to avoid the danger of the audit reflecting the narrow perceptions and interests of a single expert or group of experts from the same field.

3.18 FLOW CHARTS

Flow charts can form a very useful aid to risk identification, both by indicating potentially vulnerable areas in the company's operations and by suggesting questions to be asked during site visits. A flow chart depicts the way materials and products move through the organisation from original suppliers to final customers. The chart may be superimposed on a site plan, which will give basic information about the layout of the operations and can be useful in identifying points where hazardous operations may involve risk for nearby stages of the operation and also such risks as those caused by potential traffic congestion. Flow charts may, however, be purely schematic as in the example below.

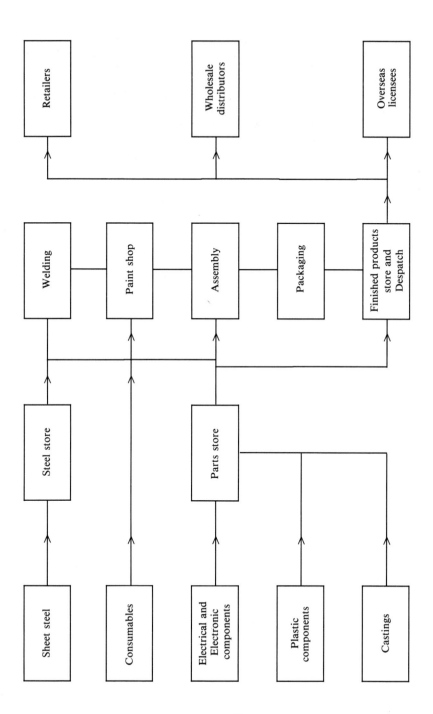

Fig. 2 : Schematic Flowchart — Machine Manufacture (simplified)

3.19   Charts such as this are particularly useful in identifying concentrations of materials and areas through which large quantities of materials must pass, thereby indicating those aspects of the operations which are particularly important for the company's flow of earnings. They omit, however, some very important information about the values involved at each stage of the process. For this reason, it is preferable to construct a quantified flow chart, such as that below, which, by showing the value added at each stage of the process and the cumulative values, enables the effect of stoppages at any point of the process to be calculated in terms of lost earnings. As is so often the case, the process of risk identification is thus combined with that of risk measurement.

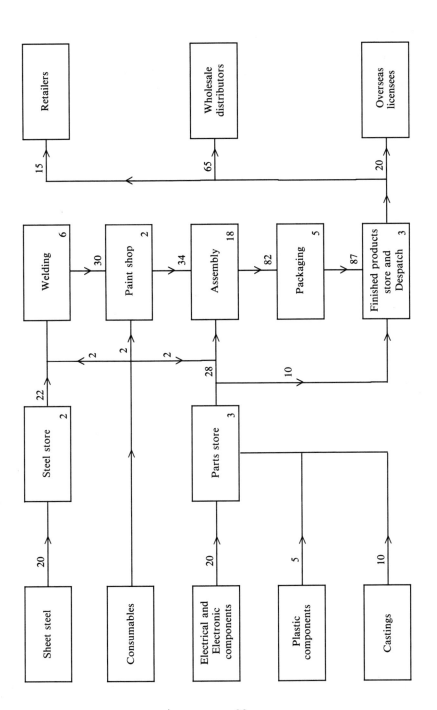

Fig. 3 : Quantified Flowchart — Machine Manufacture [Figures = % of Final Value]

3.20   INPUT-OUTPUT ANALYSIS

A quantified flow chart presents the succession and interdependency of different departments or operational stages of the company in graphical form. The same information can be expressed in tabular form, so that the key areas on which the company depends can be identified. The quantified flow chart above can be expressed in the form of an input-output matrix as follows:

INPUTS / OUTPUTS	SHEET STEEL	CONSUMABLES	ELECTRICAL & ELECTRONIC COMPONENTS	PLASTIC COMPONENTS	CASTINGS	STEEL STORE	PARTS STORE	WELDING	PAINT SHOP	ASSEMBLY	PACKAGING	FINISHED PRODUCTS STORE & DESPATCH		RETAILERS	DISTRIBUTORS	OVERSEAS LICENSEES	TOTAL
SHEET STEEL						20											20
CONSUMABLES								2	2	2							6
ELECTRICAL & ELECTRONIC COMPONENTS							20										20
PLASTIC COMPONENTS							5										5
CASTINGS							10										10
STEEL STORE								22									22
PARTS STORE										28		10					38
WELDING									30								30
PAINT SHOP										34							34
ASSEMBLY											82						82
PACKAGING												87					87
FINISHED PRODUCTS STORE & DESPATCH														15	65	20	100
NET INPUT						20	35	24	32	64	82	97		15	65	20	
VALUE ADDED						2	3	6	2	18	5	3		–	–	–	
TOTAL INPUT						22	38	30	34	82	87	100		15	65	20	

Fig. 4 : Input-Output Matrix

3.21 SITE VISITS

The information gathered by desk research must be supplemented, wherever possible, by first-hand information derived from site visits. There is no substitute for the risk manager seeing the key locations and meeting those who are directly concerned with the risks there. Such visits enable the risk manager:

1. — to form a view about the reliability of the documentary evidence avail-
able. In many companies, the formal reports which the risk manager studies may describe the organisation as it should operate rather than as it operates in fact. By "going to see", the risk manager can observe the extent to which standard practices are subject to local variation, the extent to which "temporary" variations are permitted to persist, and the local attitude to loss control and learn much that will never appear in any report.

2. — to speak to those who are close to the risks and to hear their views, which may suggest other aspects of risk which would not otherwise be identified.

3. — to build up the informal network of contacts which will be necessary to supplement official reporting channels if the risk manager is to be confident of being kept informed of new risks and of changes in existing risks.

CHAPTER 4

RISK MEASUREMENT

4.1   Just as no action can be taken to manage a risk until it has been identified, so the choice of the correct action to be taken depends upon proper measurement of the risk. Measurement is of two kinds:

(i)   Measurement of probability;

(ii)   Measurement of potential severity.

There is a link between these two measurements in that as the probability increases, so the severity tends to decrease, and vice versa. This is not an invariable rule, but the relationship holds good sufficiently often for it to be possible, if one has been able to measure probability or severity, to make a first estimate of the other.

4.2   **MEASURING PROBABILITY**

This is usually the more difficult of the two to measure accurately. The risks facing a company are not of a kind where the number of possible outcomes are known for certain, so that a statistical probability can be exactly calculated. All that can be done is to calculate a probability of future occurrences based on information about the past. The probability arrived at will never be more than an estimate, but, because of the operation of the **law of large numbers**, the greater the body of relevant data on which the prediction is based, the more closely the predicted frequency will approach the true probability of occurrence.

4.3   Two important conclusions follow from this:

(i)   The better the records that have been kept of past occurrences of a similar kind, the better the measurement of the probability of a particular risk is likely to be;

(ii)   Because they happen so infrequently compared with small losses, the information available about catastrophic events is likely to be very limited, so that measurement of the probability of such events, which are the ones about which the risk manager will be most concerned, is likely to be the least exact.

4.4   The measurement of probability cannot be divorced from questions of severity, because the information most useful to the risk manager will not be the simple probability of a particular risk occurring, but the probability of it producing effects which would seriously affect the business. The most accurate determination of the probability of a fire occurring is of little use if the prediction does not distinguish between say, a trivial fire in a waste-paper basket and one which destroys a factory. In attempting to fit past data to a probability distribution which will enable predictions to be made about future probability, therefore, it is essential to group the data into classes by the size of the loss caused. It may be convenient to arrange for these classes to match the financial levels which decide whether a loss for the particular organisation in its current financial state is to be considered trivial, minor, major or catastrophic, since these divisions will largely decide the risk management method of choice for any particular risk.

4.5   Probability is expressed as a number on a scale between 0 and 1, where 0 means that the event cannot occur and 1 means that it is certain to occur. A risk with a probability of occurrence of .75 is therefore one that is very likely to occur, since there are 75 changes in 100 that it will do so. If the probability is .001, then it can be considered an unlikely event, there being only 1 chance in 1000 that it will occur.

4.6   Even if the probability is mathematically correct, it is not an exact predictor of individual events. The probability of an event may suggest that it can be expected to occur once in 100 years, but one cannot count on there being an exact interval of 100 years between such events. Two or more could occur in successive years, or even in a shorter period, without invalidating the probability calculation. Probabilities can thus be useful on setting priorities for action about risk, but one must be careful in using them as reasons for deciding to take no action.

4.7   THE POISSON DISTRIBUTION

Of the various probability distributions which may represent the pattern of losses of the organisation, the Poisson distribution is likely to be of particular interest to the risk manager, and it offers the possibility, if an expected number of losses can be determined on the basis of past data, of predicting the probability of any specific number of losses, and of indicating a figure which can, for practical purposes, be taken as the maximum number of losses.

4.8   By using the formula

$$\frac{e^{-n} \, n^r}{r!}$$

where e is the constant   2.7183

n is the expected number of losses based on past data

and r is the number of losses for which a probability prediction is required,

the probability of there being any specific number of losses can be calculated. The probability of there being more than a specific number of losses can be found by totalling the probabilities for 0 losses and for each whole number up to and including the required figure, and subtracting that total from 1 (since the sum of the probabilities of all possible outcomes must equal 1 (or certainty).

4.9 When the probability given by this formula approaches 0 and becomes sufficiently small to be discounted for practical purposes, one can consider that number of events as the maximum that can reasonably be expected. One should note, however, that this does not mean that the event is impossible, and it should be disregarded only to the extent that there are other risks with a higher priority for management.

4.10 MEASURING SEVERITY

The purpose of measuring a risk is primarily to be able to locate it in the scale of risks facing an organisation. Only if this is done can priorities for action be assigned, the correct type of risk management action determined and the effect of any risk reduction be calculated.

4.11 The risks facing an organisation can be divided into four types, depending upon the effect they would have upon the organisation if they were to occur. These are:

① — **Trivial risks** — whose effects the organisation can bear without difficulty as part of its normal operations.

② — **Minor risks** — whose effects can be borne within a single accounting period provided the number of events does not become excessive.

③ — **Major risks** — whose effects would be too great for the organisation to bear in a single accounting period, but which would become acceptable if the cost could be spread over a sufficient period of time.

④ — **Catastrophic risks** — whose effects would destroy the organisation.

For any given organisation, the divisions between these categories can be expressed in financial terms. The amounts involved will, however, vary for each organisation, since what is a major risk for a small business may rank as trivial for an multinational company, and even for the same organisation at different times, as its financial situation changes.

4.12 As mentioned above, there tends to be an inverse ratio between the size of a risk and its frequency, so that the majority of risks will fall into the 'trivial' and minor categories, with the frequency of major risks being relatively small and the catastrophic ones being rare.

This can be illustrated as follows:

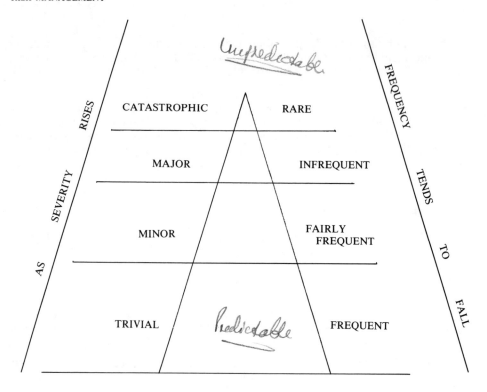

Fig. 5

4.13   Measurement of severity for risk management purposes must be distinguish-ed from the fixing of sums insured and limits of liability for insurance purposes, which has to be done in the context of the insurance cover available and its exclu-sions, and with uninsurable items, which include many of the indirect costs of a loss, omitted. In trying to assess the potential severity of a risk, all the conse-quences, direct and indirect must be taken into consideration. Furthermore, property accidents may involve injuries and both may involve an interruption to the business or possibility of incurring liability, so that calculating the overall severity of a risk may involve totalling costs of many different kinds. The two main questions to be asked are:

1 — what is the maximum aggregate of losses which might arise from one event or a related series of events?

2 — what is the minimum amount of resources the organisation will need, following such a loss, if it is to continue to meet its objectives.

30

4.14   Calculation of potential losses will often require assistance from experts of all kinds, from accountants, architects, surveyors, valuers, engineers, lawyers and insurance advisers among others. It is not a job that a single risk manager can be expected to carry out unaided.

4.15   MEASUREMENT OF POTENTIAL PROPERTY LOSSES

In general, the insurance approach to quantifying potential property losses is based on determining the cost of replacing or reinstating property lost or damaged, but the risk manager is more concerned with determining the cost of replacing the flow of earnings that the property represents. Viewed in this light, replacement or reinstatement may not necessarily be the best course of action. As an example, a food firm, which suffered a serious fire at one of its major production units, decided that the most effective way of minimising the production loss was not to set about speedy replacement of the damaged plant, but to acquire a smaller company nearby which was engaged in the same type of business.

4.16   Replacement will usually be the most effective way of dealing with losses of **raw materials, work in progress and finished stocks**, and their value for risk management purposes will be the cost of replacing them at a similar state of manufacture, plus the cost of any delay involved in doing so. Irreplaceable items should be accorded the present value of the future earnings they represent, but, by forethought and good risk management practice, it will often be possible to reduce the amount that is irreplaceable by duplication of sources, by buffer stocks or even by changes to production practices.

4.17   Determining a value for **capital assets** is much more difficult. The cost to the organisation of being deprived of their use may well vary according to what it would do if it lost them. Once again, the inter-relation of various stages of risk management is well illustrated here, because, in order to measure the risk effectively, one needs to consider what action would be taken in the event of each type of major loss, in other words, to have developed an adequate contingency plan. One of the important benefits of a risk management approach to the quantification of potential losses may well be to reveal the need to plan ahead for disaster.

4.18   As an example, suppose that a soft drinks firm is attempting to quantify the risk of losing the bottling plant for one of its long-established products. The cost of replacing the plant and the associated indirect costs may be ascertainable, but this is only the cost of the risk if replacement would be the chosen option in the event of loss. But there would be other possibilities, such as:

— sub-contracting the bottling;

— franchising the bottling to local bottlers round the country;

— utilising spare capacity at other plants, or extending them to meet the extra demand;

— taking the opportunity to phase out the old product and to launch an new, more fashionable and more profitable product in its place.

4.19   Each course of action would involve a different cost, so that only if the probable choice is known is it possible to determine the potential severity of the risk. With some choices, the risk might be classified as a major one for the company, but with others, particularly the last option, which involves speculative risks which would themselves have to be analysed, the risk might prove to be of minor severity only.

4.20   Threats to particular assets should not be quantified in isolation. One must always consider what else could be lost or damaged at the same time, and whether any probable combination would imply a major interruption to the operations of the organisation, or serious liabilities being incurred, which could turn a major loss into a disaster.

4.21   Potential **liability risks** are particularly difficult to quantify. Where the claim arises from damage to property, the problem may be eased by such factors as:

— limits of liability set by statute, custom of trade or contract;

— the possibility of determining an approximate total value of the property of others capable of being affected by such events as a serious fire or explosion on one's own premises.

— assessment of the value of property or premises of others which are being worked on.

4.22   Where personal injury is involved, whether to employees, customers or other members of the public, the problem is much greater, because each occurrence of liability has a unique cost, which has ultimately to be set by the courts (or by negotiations which are implicitly based on what the courts would award), and the only ceiling to which, in theory at least, is the total worth of the organisation liable.

4.23   To be able to estimate the potential cost of such a liability risk one must therefore be aware of the current level of court awards, not only in the home country of the organisation, but wherever it has premises or its products may be used. One must always err on the side of pessimism when considering the numbers of people who may be injured or killed. The past may, in this as in all things, not be a sufficiently accurate guide to the future. Until the Bhopal disaster, for example, with its thousands of victims, the maximum number of people known to have been injured by a single escape of toxic gas from industrial premises was about 60.

4.24 BUSINESS INTERRUPTION LOSSES

Any interruption to the operations of a business involves a cost, but an organisation which has well-prepared contingency plans, and therefore has a clear idea of the steps necessary to take in order to minimise the effect and duration of the interruption will be better-placed to calculate the true cost of the interruption, whether caused by events at the organisation's own premises or by the inability of suppliers to provide materials or of customers to accept finished products.

This cost will be made up of:

— Loss of profit derived from the revenue lost during the stoppage;

— Additional costs incurred to maintain operations;

— Additional costs incurred to minimise the recovery period.

4.25   The extent to which additional costs have to be incurred will depend upon the type of organisation involved, the nature and competitiveness of its market, and the uniqueness of its products. Normal cost-benefit calculations will be applied to such expenditure, but where absence from the marketplace could mean a permanent loss of market share, or where the objective of the organisation is the provision of an important public service, it may be necessary to incur expenditure which is 'uneconomic' in the short term.

4.26 LOSSES BY DISHONESTY

In measuring risks of this kind, whether the dishonesty occurs within the organisation or outside, one must try to determine what is the maximum amount of cash or property that one person or group of persons acting in concert could make away with. Where single thefts are concerned, it may be relatively easy to put a maximum figure on the loss, but internal frauds involving cash or stock may be carried out over a very long period and can assume major proportions. Remember, too, that this is an area in which information about the past may be very misleading, since it is only the frauds which were ultimately unsuccessful that will appear in the records.

4.27 CREDIT RISKS

Here the total value at risk will be the value of outstanding debts owed to the organisation, plus the value of any stock manufactured to a customer's specification and awaiting delivery for which there would be no ready alternative market.

4.28 AGGREGATE LOSSES

It is important not to consider separate types of potential loss in isolation when measuring risk. The total cost of loss will be the aggregate of all types of loss arising from the same cause. The more types of loss that are involved, the more difficult it will be to produce an accurate cost of risk, and planning appropriate risk handling methods may be eased if a range of possible severities is considered. Thus one might consider:

1 — a <u>worst</u> case, assuming that everything possible went wrong;

2 — a case of <u>moderate</u> severity, which represents the best estimate of probable loss;

3 — a case of <u>low</u> severity, where the loss occurred, but most things went in one's favour.

It is important to remember that the aggregate loss may be out of all proportion to the size of the primary loss. Thus the failure of a tiny component in a key piece of equipment could bring about substantial property damage, injury to employees and third parties, pollution of the surrounding area, prolonged business interruption and large liability claims.

4.29   ACCUMULATION OF LOSSES

So far, we have been concerned with estimating the cost of a single occurrence of a loss. While one can generalise and say that trivial risks will be common, minor losses fairly frequent, major losses uncommon and catastrophic losses rare, one must never forget:

— that the occurrence of individual losses from pure risks is random;

— that unpredictability tends to increase with severity.

The predicted frequency of a particular type of loss might be only one occurrence in three hundred years, but it is entirely possible that there could be two such losses in as many years, or even two in one month. In measuring risk, therefore, it is necessary not only to consider the potential cost of each occurrence, but also to go further and to calculate how many such losses could be borne in a single year's operations before assigning the risk to a severity category and deciding upon the appropriate treatment for the risk.

CHAPTER 5

RISK AVOIDANCE AND REDUCTION

5.01 RISK AVOIDANCE

The problems associated with risk can be solved by taking action to avoid the risk. Depending on the type of risk involved, this can be achieved by:

— ceasing the activity which brings about the risk;

— changing the location at which it is done;

— changing the materials used;

— changing the method by which it is done.

5.02 The opportunities for such action are, however, limited. Ceasing an operation eliminates the risks associated with it, but it also deprives the organisation of the profit derived from it. Changing the location may be impracticable if it would mean moving a major production plant with all the associated capital expenditure. There may be no alternative process or materials which would provide an acceptable product. Risk avoidance, therefore, tends to involve unacceptable levels of disruption or expense.

5.03 Action taken to avoid risk, like any other risk management action, will have an effect on the risk pattern. One specific risk may be avoided, but the probability or potential severity of others may be changed by the avoiding action, and new risks may be created. One might, for example, avoid a risk of fire by ceasing to use a flammable material, but the replacement material introduced might create a toxic hazard.

5.04 Risk avoidance is common with speculative risks, because once the benefits and risks of a new project have been considered, there is usually a point at which a decision whether or not to proceed is taken, usually at a high level within the organisation. An unacceptable level of risk would be a reason for deciding against proceeding with the project, and this decision avoids the risk. Unfortunately, such a procedure is less common where pure risks are concerned. Often it is only after the project is under way, the factory location chosen, or the process designed that thought is given to managing the pure risks. If, however, they too are considered at the design or planning stage, risk avoidance becomes a real option. Avoidance of, for example, a flood risk is feasible when locations for a potential new plant are being considered but may cease to be so once the plant has been constructed and its removal would mean unacceptable interruption and cost.

5.05 RISK REDUCTION

Since risk avoidance is only of limited use as a risk management strategy, a more common approach to the treatment of risk is to seek to reduce it. Reduction may be of either probability or severity, and may take effect before, during or after a loss. The various stages may be set out thus:

Stage	Technique	Aim
1 Pre-loss	Prevention	Reduce Probability (Risk reduction)
2 During loss	Protection Salvage	Reduce Severity (Loss reduction)
3 Post-loss	Recovery Programme	Reduce Severity (Loss Reduction)

5.06 All forms of risk and loss reduction will involve the use of the following:

- Human action;
- Physical measures;
- Organisational measures;
- Educational measures;
- Financial resources.

5.07 HUMAN ACTION

Properly trained, motivated and directed, people are the most effective means at the disposal of the risk manager in reducing risk or its effects. Everyone in an organisation has the power to increase its vulnerability to risk or to play a part in risk management.

5.08 In addition to the first line of defence, which is made up of the talents, expertise and efforts of the members of the organisation itself, there is the contribution that can be made to risk management by experts of all kinds. No one person can be sufficiently well aware of all the vast range of risks facing any organisation and of the best techniques for countering them. The help of outside experts must therefore be sought. At the same time, one must be conscious that leaving risk matters entirely to the expert may involve some dangers:

— The presence of the expert may be an excuse for no-one else to give any thought to the risk. Risk management is most effective when everyone is involved.

— Experts have an understandable tendency to be proud of their expertise, and will tend to concentrate on identifying risk problems and proposing solutions to them which call for the use of that expertise. If things are left entirely to them, simple risks which do not call for highly technical methods of control may be overlooked.

— As a specialist dealing with a specific problem, the expert may not consider the effect which his recommended solution will itself have upon the organisation's overall risk pattern, especially the risks which the solution itself may create.

5.09   PHYSICAL MEASURES

Under this heading come all the physical devices designed to prevent loss or to limit its effects. The following are a few examples:

Fire and explosion risks :	smoke detectors, sprinklers, explosion suppression;
Safety:	machine guards, interlocks, protective clothing;
Security:	intruder alarms, perimeter fencing;
Dishonesty risks:	armoured glass at cash counters, closed circuit television;
Liability risks:	metal detectors on food production lines; ultrasonic testing;
Pollution:	exhaust gas scrubbers; effluent control machinery.

5.10   Physical loss control systems are of two kinds:

— **active systems** which operate permanently to detect the occurrence of a loss and/or to prevent it or limit its effects. Detectors and alarms of all kinds come into this category.

— **passive systems** which are triggered by the loss itself. Examples of this type of system are fire shutters and automatic extinguishing systems of all kinds.

5.11   ORGANISATIONAL MEASURES

Physical risk reduction measures are most effective if they are backed up with organisational methods which ensure that operations are carried on in a way which minimises risk. This is not only a matter of making sure that the organisation complies with legal requirements such as those contained in fire regulations for buildings and processes, but also of arranging operations in a way that seeks to make it easier to prevent loss than to cause it. Risk reduction, to be effective, must be part of the routine, not an inconvenient interruption to it.

5.12   Organisational methods of risk reduction will include such things as:

- operating procedures which minimise risk, such as "permit to work" systems for non-routine operations involving hazards;

- access control measures;

- smoking restrictions;

- systems to ensure correct labelling of products;

- controls on disposal of wastes and effluents.

5.13   EDUCATIONAL MEASURES

The human resources which the organisation can use to reduce risk which only be effective if they have the necessary training, and education in risk control measures should be part of all risk management programmes. Management and staff should be taught to be aware:

- that risk exists;

- that it poses a threat to the continuance of the organisation;

- that something can be done about it;

- that it is everyone's job to help reduce the threat;

- of how to reduce the effect of specific risks by knowing what to do, where to go and whom to notify in the event of an emergency.

5.14   FINANCIAL RESOURCES

Risk reduction costs money, and so there must be a budget for this stage of risk management. It will, however, be in competition for the allocation of financial resources with other projects, and while it may be thought desirable to spend money on reducing risk, few organisations will be in a position to allot the risk management programme all the money that it could use in this field. Expenditure on loss control, like any other, must be justified by the benefits to be expected, and the organisation's financial situation may preclude installing all the physical risk reduction devices that it would ideally have. Wise use of the budget allocated will be called for, and this may mean concentration on organisational methods and training, which can often make up for the absence of automatic risk reduction devices.

5.15 FIRE PREVENTION

Fire is a major risk for most organisations, and the risk of fire is one where reduction often involves the use of physical measures. Automatic systems can be used to detect the start of a fire and to extinguish it before it has a chance to grow to major proportions. The proper use of human resources and organisational means can also be of very great help in reducing the risk of loss by fire. The following chart sets out examples of the different kinds of resources available to an organisation in countering the risk of fire:

Resources	Pre-Loss Prevention	Time of Loss Protection	Salvage	Post-Loss Recovery
Human	Fire prevention engineers	Fire prevention engineers	Salvage teams	Contingency plan controller
	Security patrols	Fire brigades	First aiders	Risk manager
	Risk manager			
Physical	Fire separation	Sprinklers	Smoke removal	Alternative plant or premises
	Flameproofing	Extinguishers	Sheeting	
		Fire doors		
Organisational	Maintenance	Loss limitation procedures	Emergency procedures	Recovery plan
	Housekeeping		Orderly evacuation	
	Supervision			
Educational	Awareness training	------------- Training put into practice -------------		
	Practice drills			
Financial	Loss control budget	Loss control budget		Contingency reserves
				CL insurance

5.16 SAFETY

Since human life is at stake, there are additional reasons for effective control of risk. The three incentives for loss control activity are:

① — **legal requirements**

② — **humanitarian considerations**

③ — **economic considerations**

5.17 LEGISLATION

Complying with safety legislation is the minimum level of loss prevention. In the United Kingdom, the main legislation is contained in the Health and Safety at Work etc. Act 1974. This imposes a general duty on employers to provide safe premises and plant. Associated regulations and codes of practice lay down specific rules for the safe operation of particular processes and plant and the use of certain materials, and the Health and Safety Inspectorate enforce observance of the legislation, with power to issue improvement notices, requiring safety to be improved within a certain period or prohibition notices requiring an operation to be suspended until it can be carried out with an acceptable degree of safety. The Act also imposes a duty upon employees to have regard for their own safety and that of their fellow-employees and others who may be affected by the work. CIMAH (Control of Industrial Major Hazards) and COSHH (Control of Substances Hazardous to Health) Regulations effectively make some elements of risk management compulsory for installations with particular safety hazards.

5.18 HUMANITARIAN CONSIDERATIONS

Merely to comply with the law is unlikely to be sufficient since it is a standardised duty, while loss prevention must be adapted to the individual organisation. The legal minimum will also be increased by the extent to which each organisation feels a responsibility to its workforce, which, in turn, will be a reflection of its response to the social environment in which the organisation operates. What is expected of a responsible employer will always move ahead of legislation, and particular features of the industry of which it forms part, such as a well-publicised disaster, will increase the minimum safety expenditure that will be expected from it.

5.19 ECONOMIC CONSIDERATIONS

In addition to what is required by the above considerations, each organisation will carry out any further loss prevention activity which is economically justified. Any accident has associated costs, both direct and indirect, which may be difficult to quantify, but which may nevertheless represent a serious loss. There is thus a financial incentive to reduce loss.

5.20 ACCIDENT RATIOS

Studies of large numbers of accidents, notably by two American researchers, Heinrich and Bird, indicate that a ratio can be shown to exist between totals of accidents of different severities. This means that any action taken which reduces the number of minor accidents or 'near misses', where all the circumstances for an accident were present, but no injury or property damage in fact occurred, will automatically reduce the number of more serious accidents. It is therefore more effective to attempt to reduce the number of minor accidents, about the cause and circumstances of which, because of their frequency, there is likely to be much more information available. The necessity of maintaining adequate records is clear.

5.21 SECURITY

The approach to all loss control will differ depending upon whether one is dealing with **fortuitous loss** or with **deliberately-caused loss**. Where the former is concerned, one knows that once the risk has been foreseen and the necessary loss prevention measures introduced, then provided the system operates as it should, the problem has been solved, because the force producing the loss will not change. Where one is facing a loss brought about by a deliberate act, one cannot make this assumption. Because the effective force is directed by a human mind, it can always be modified to overcome any protections. Security is a field where this type of loss has to be dealt with, and one may find that the better the protections that are introduced, the more of a challenge they may present to someone determined to overcome them. Loss prevention systems and devices need therefore to be continually monitored, not only to check that they are still operating, but also to see whether they need to be changed.

5.22   The losses that security systems must guard against may be motivated by gain, revenge, political or social protest or simply by the pleasure taken in destruction. Theft of money, goods or information is the main crime involved but the risks of vandalism, arson, and terrorism have also to be faced. The loss prevention approach will vary, however, depending upon whether it is **opportunity crime** or **planned crime**, which has to be deterred approach.

5.23 OPPORTUNITY CRIME

Some losses come about simply because it is easy to commit them. They are easily deterred by simple loss prevention devices. Because little planning commonly goes into them, they are likely to be of low severity, and extensive efforts to eliminate them cannot usually be justified on economic grounds. Minor acts of shoplifting, pilferage and vandalism are typical losses of this kind. Many businesses accept that they will happen and build the cost into operating budgets. Some loss prevention may be justified, however, to prevent the number of such events becoming so large as to constitute a significant loss in total.

5.24 PLANNED CRIME

This type of loss can reach major proportions, and requires a much greater loss prevention effort. The systems to be used are of two kinds: those that **control people** and those that **control objects**. Physical barriers may keep intruders out, but organisational means and supervision will be the key to security systems on the premises. Losses do not always originate outside. People legitimately on the premises: employees, visitors, contractors' staff and others, may themselves be responsible for losses or make them possible. Access control, whether by physical barriers alarms and detectors or operational systems which make it difficult for people to enter particular parts of the premises unless it is necessary for their work will reduce risk, but they will depend upon accurate identification of the key vulnerabilities of the organisation. Limiting accumulations of goods attractive to thieves and dispersing the storage of key information may reduce the risk of a major loss, although by creating more locations to be protected it may increase the probability of a smaller loss.

5.25 POLITICAL CRIME

This presents particular problems because, as its aim is normally destruction or disruption, there is less restraint about how it is caused and less concern about casualties. Other crime threatens property rather than people, and although there may be injury, this is incidental to the main purpose. With political crime it may itself be the purpose. The key to loss prevention here is to be aware of the political and social environment in which one operates and of the features of one's organisation which might make it a target for such risks, and, in the light of this information to install appropriate security equipment and to plan, and above all to practise, procedures to reduce the risk.

5.26 LIABILITY LOSS CONTROL

The risk of incurring substantial liabilities has for many organisations become the biggest single risk it faces, and it is the one where loss reduction presents the biggest problem. This is because:

- (1)— virtually everyone in the organisation can bring about a liability loss;

- (2)— liability may arise in connection with almost anything an organisation does, has done for it, or fails to do;

- (3)— there need be no correlation between the apparent seriousness of the event or action which triggers off the liability and the size of the loss.

5.27 Many liabilities arise in connection with injury to persons or damage to property. Where such injury or damage could arise in circumstances which are under the organisation's immediate control, then clearly any action taken to prevent the injury or damage will automatically reduce the liability as well. Where the accident occurs beyond that control, as is usually the case with products liability, or where economic loss is concerned, as with some professional liabilities, this advantage is lost. Apart from physical quality control and inspection measures to reduce the products liability risk in some industries, all loss control for losses of these kinds has to be by organisational means. Design must limit the possibilities of malfunction or misuse of products, systems must be put in place to ensure that packaging and instructions are correct and appropriate for the market being supplied, and the method of dealing with complaints must be such that a minimum of them develop into claims. Where professional risks are concerned, organisational controls must be devised to limit the possibility of incorrect advice being given, to ensure that members of the organisation do not go beyond the areas which they are qualified to advise, and, wherever it is possible to do so, to use appropriate and adequate disclaimers.

42

5.28 EVALUATING LOSS CONTROL OPTIONS

All loss control measures cost money, and any that go beyond what is legally required and what the organisation recognises as expected of it by society, will have to compete with other projects for the organisation's resources. They may start with the disadvantage of appearing rather unexciting and negative when in competition with other schemes which offer a direct increase in profit for the organisation, and it will be part of the task of the risk manager to educate management into accepting that reduction of the cost of risk can itself improve profitability. Demonstrating this advantage of loss reduction will, however, require the application of **cost-benefit** analysis to the loss reduction schemes proposed.

5.29   The costs and the benefits of loss reduction will include both direct and indirect considerations, which will often be difficult to quantify exactly. The largest benefit, for example, will be represented by the losses which are prevented or the reduction in the cost of those which do occur, so that one can never put an exact value on it. The following are some of the elements which might appear in the cost-benefit analysis:

Direct costs

Cost of loss reduction equipment

Cost of improved construction

Equipment maintenance costs

Cost of improved housekeeping & supervision

Cost of education in loss prevention

Direct benefits

− Savings through losses which do not occur

— Insurance premium discounts for installing equipment

— Future premium savings through improved experience

Indirect costs

Interference with operations while installing, maintaining & testing equipment.

Interference with operations by equipment itself

− when functioning

− when malfunctioning

Indirect benefits

− Improved productivity by avoiding disruption of losses.

− Improved industrial relations

— Public relations benefits

5.30   Presentation of risk reduction projections will have to be made in terms comparable with those used for considering any other proposal requiring funds. Frequently there may be alternative ways of achieving the desired reduction and a choice has to be made between them. The simplest method to apply is that of comparing the **payback** period, i.e. calculating how long it will take the project to recover in savings the cost that it entails. The drawback of this method is that it takes no account of any savings which may be made after the project has paid back its costs. Thus an option with a short payback period but nothing to offer thereafter could be chosen in preference to one which offers a longer payback period but also a continuing flow of savings.

5.31   In order to take account of all the savings offered for the entire period the organisation considers when deciding whether the cost of a project is justified, one might use the **accounting rate of return method**, by which the cost of each competing project is divided by its total return. The project showing the highest ratio of return to cost would be selected.

5.32   Neither of these methods, however, makes allowance for the time value of money. A return which will only be received in five years' time is not as valuable to an organisation as the same amount receivable immediately. One way of overcoming this problem in assessing the return from a loss reduction (or any other) project is by the use of the net present value (NPV) method of **discounted cash flow**, by which future expenses and benefits can be expressed in terms of their equivalent value in present terms, taking into account the length of time that will elapse before they are paid or received. The discount rate used in the calculation represents what it would cost the organisation to borrow or the return it could expect to obtain by investing money in the period between the present and the expected date of payment or receipt.

5.33   Let us suppose that we are calculating the net present value of a project to install fire prevention equipment which will cost £50,000 but which it is expected will provide the following savings in insurance premiums and other costs over the next five years, which is the period over which the organisation evaluates capital expenditure proposals. It is assumed that the outlay will be made immediately, but that the benefits will accrue at the end of each year, and the discount rate chosen is 10%:

Year	Cost	Benefit
1	£50,000	£18,000
2	–	£18,000
3	–	£18,000
4	–	£12,000
5	–	£10,000

The formula for the calculation is:

$$NPV = (-C) + a_1(1+i)^{-1} + a_2(1+i)^{-2} + a_3(1+i)^{-3} \ldots\ldots\ldots a_n(1+i)^{-n}$$

where C is the capital outlay; a_1, a_2, a_3 .....a_n are the returns in years 1, 2, 3 .... year n; and i is the discount rate.

In our example, therefore, the net present value will be:

$(-£50,000) + (£18,000 \times 1.1^{-1}) + (£18,000 \times 1.1^{-2}) + (£18,000 \times 1.1^{-3})$
$+ (£12,000 \times 1.1^{-4}) + (£10,000 \times 1.1^{-5})$

$$
\begin{array}{llll}
= (-£50,000) & + & £18,000 \times \dfrac{1}{1.1} & = £16,363.64 \\[3mm]
& + & £18,000 \times \dfrac{1}{1.1^2} & = £14,876.03 \\[3mm]
& + & £18,000 \times \dfrac{1}{1.1^3} & = £13,523.67 \\[3mm]
& + & £12,000 \times \dfrac{1}{1.1^4} & = £\ 8,196.16 \\[3mm]
& + & £10,000 \times \dfrac{1}{1.1^5} & = £\ 6,209.21 \\[3mm]
& & & \overline{£59,168.71} \\
& & \text{Less} & £50,000.00 \\
& & & \overline{} \\
& \text{NPV} & & = £\ 9,168.71
\end{array}
$$

5.34 CONTINGENCY PLANNING

Loss reduction is only one stage in the wider-ranging concept of contingency planning. It would, in fact, be reasonable to consider the whole of risk management to be an exercise in contingency planning, identifying possible disasters, and deciding what can be done to reduce their probability or severity and to decide, in advance, what action to take if they should arise, so that the effect on the smooth running of the organisation is minimised. This approach is based on recognition of the following:

— that many organisations are driven out of business by the interruption caused by risks which they should have been able to control / identify

— that the secret of survival when faced with disaster is to have a well-thought-out plan;

— that it is easier to draw up a plan in advance, when proper time and thought can be given to the exercise than to make sound decisions in the stress and confusion caused by the emergency.

— that the planning exercise itself will identify potential disasters and ways to prevent them.

45

5.35   Contingency planning prepares the organisation for three phases of action:

— **pre-loss**: when the emphasis is on ways of preventing the risk from producing its effects, and ensuring that those effects are minimised if the loss does occur.

— **time of loss**: when the main concerns are to save life and salvage property, and to bring the disaster to an end as quickly and safely as possible, so as to limit its effects.

— **post-loss**: when a recovery plan will be implemented to bring the organisation back to its normal pre-loss level of operations as quickly as possible.

5.36   The loss control techniques discussed earlier in this chapter are the tools upon which the pre-loss stage of the contingency plan depends, and some of them will come into effect to limit the loss at the time it occurs. Once the disaster happens, however, new techniques must be ready for use, based upon a realistic assessment of what might happen in spite of all precautions and on a full understanding of what materials, resources and services the organisation will require to overcome the emergency. The aim must be to end the emergency situation as quickly as possible, so that the recovery plan can begin to be put into effect.

5.37   The essentials of disaster and recovery planning can be summed up as **collection of information** and **allocation of responsibilities**. The basic idea of planning is to decide in advance what needs to be done, who should do it and what information that person needs to act effectively. This means that the first stage in contingency planning is to decide what circumstances would constitute an emergency for which a contingency plan would be needed. This cannot be done by each department of the organisation working in isolation. Everything that one department does in an emergency has an effect on other departments, and to create what amounts to a series of separate plans is a recipe for increasing the chaos caused by an emergency. For example, a purchasing department might look for suppliers of alternative raw materials for use if the organisation were deprived of its stockpile, but this would be no use if the production department had decided that in the same circumstances it would switch to alternative machinery which could not handle the alternative materials chosen.

5.38   It is also necessary to decide what the organisation would in fact wish to do if its operations were brought to a sudden stop by a disaster. Swift re-establishment of what went before might not be the best course to follow, and the organisation might wish to use the interruption positively and take the opportunity to change the way it operates. Unless thought is given to possibilities of this kind, it is clear that any contingency plan decided on may not be the most effective one.

5.39   INFORMATION

The key to good decision making is the right information. When an emergency occurs, information will be needed about sources of assistance and suppliers of temporary and replacement premises, equipment, materials and staff, and services of all kinds. The basic research is much more effectively carried out before the emergency arises, but the information collected must be recorded in a form which will be available when it is needed and regularly updated.

5.40   RESPONSIBILITIES

The plan must also spell out who is responsible for deciding when circumstances warrant the plan being put into action, and who is to take control of the various actions decided upon to limit the effects of the emergency and to restore normality. Deputies should be nominated, to avoid confusion if individuals given responsibilities are absent at the time of the disaster, or are among its victims. The list of responsibilities must be kept up to date and those on it should be familiar with what will be expected of them. It will be too late for them to start thinking of what is entailed once the emergency has arisen.

5.41   MEDIA COMMUNICATIONS

If a major disaster is involved, there is certain to be press, radio and television interest and the responsibility for representing the organisation has become one of the most important to be decided upon. The way in which press relations are handled can have a significant influence upon the public image of the organisation, which in turn may be a factor in deciding whether or not it will survive the disaster.

5.42   PRACTICE

Except for particularly hazardous sites, where a simulated disaster exercise involving local authorities and emergency services may have to be carried out, it is unlikely that many organisations will be able to afford the time and expense of a full-scale test of the contingency plan, but anything that can be done, even in such relatively simple measures as fire drills, evacuation exercises and in training staff to use the loss prevention equipment provided will be worthwhile. Even if the contingency plan is never put into action in a real emergency, it will have served a useful purpose if, in the course of drawing it up, the organisation has been forced to think seriously and constructively about what it would do in the event of an emergency, because the exercise itself may give it a greater insight into the risks it faces and what can be done about them. This may give the incentive to take preventive action so that the disaster does not happen.

47

CHAPTER 6

RISK TRANSFER

6.01 Risk transfer can be carried out in two ways:

① — by **transferring the risk itself** to another party, which, if carried out successfully, amounts to a form of risk avoidance;

② — by **transferring the financial consequences of the risk** to another party. As this does nothing about the risk itself, it amounts to a form of financing of a retained risk.

6.02 TRANSFERRING THE RISK

It is quite common for an organisation to have some part of its operations carried out by another body on its behalf. A manufacturing process or some service may be contracted out to another party in such a way that it becomes entirely separate from the activities carried out by the organisation itself. Such arrangements are commonly entered into for financial or operational reasons, but they may also be used as a method of handling the risk which the activity entails. This may be because:

— the activity is hazardous in itself;

— the activity may not be particularly hazardous, but presents an unacceptable risk in combination with other operations;

— the activity may be unsuitable for the location in which it would have to be carried out.

① Where the activity is itself hazardous, the reason for transferring it may be a lack of the necessary expertise which a specialist contractor can provide, or the activity, while within the organisation's own capacities, may call for special safety or security precautions which it would be uneconomic for a non-specialist organisation to provide. ② In the same way, it may be prudent to transfer even a straightforward operation which presents only a moderate hazard if that hazard is one to which the organisation's own operations is particularly susceptible. Thus if most of the materials used were particularly susceptible to humidity, it might be sensible to arrange for a single wet process involving the rest of them to be carried out elsewhere by contractors.

6.03 ③ The process may be unsuitable for the organisation's own premises on many grounds. It may, for example, involve levels of noise, dust or pollution which are unacceptable locally, but which could be tolerated in a more appropriate area, the activity might be one which the organisation would prefer not to carry out itself

49

because of the adverse publicity it might create, or climatic conditions may be unsuitable for certain parts of the process.

6.04   This action may transfer the risk, but the cost of risk will of course be built into the contract price for the transfer of the activity, although a specialist contractor, because of his expertise and the volume of the work he carries out, may be able to reduce the overall cost of the risk.

6.05   TRANSFERRING THE FINANCIAL CONSEQUENCES

The most commonly-used method of risk transfer by contract is the use of insurance, which will be dealt with in Chapter 8. Apart from this, the main use of this strategy is in connection with liability risks, where attempts have frequently been made to ensure that the cost of any liability awards shall be met by a party other than the one on whom they would otherwise fall. Two principles come into conflict here, first that liability should lie where it falls, and that the person who created the liability should meet its cost, and secondly that parties to a contract should be free to negotiate whatever bargain they choose. Under growing consumer pressure, the tendency has been for the law to forbid or to restrict very severely the possibility of evading or limiting liabilities if an individual is confronted by a large organisation, where the difference of power is seen to be too great, but to permit bodies which are equal in bargaining power largely to maintain their freedom to contract on terms that suit them.

6.06   Transfer of liability risks by contract is normally attempted by **exclusion clauses**, which seek to prevent one of the parties to the contract from making a claim against the other, or by **hold harmless** or **indemnity clauses**, by which one party agrees to accept the financial consequences of a liability which would otherwise fall upon the other. It should be noted that these are contractual clauses, and therefore

1) — will be binding only on parties to the contract;

2) — to be effective, must form part of a valid contract;

3) — in the UK, they must conform to the Unfair Contract Terms Act 1977

6.07   UNFAIR CONTRACT TERMS ACT 1977

The courts have long disliked exclusion clauses of this kind, which can lead to injustice, and they therefore sought to interpret them very narrowly, and to be reluctant to enforce them if it was possible to construe the contract in such a way as to limit their effectiveness. The Unfair Contract Terms Act has limited the use of contractual clauses to limit or exclude liability even further. Section 2 of the Act prohibits restricting or contracting out of liability for personal injury through negligence whether by contract term or notice, so that this particular liability risk, which is often the most serious aspect of the potential risk of liability, cannot be transferred by contract. Liability for other loss or damage through negligence can only be restricted or excluded if the contract term or notice is reasonable.

50

6.08   The Act also prohibits the exclusion or limitation in a consumer contract, i.e. one in which one party is acting in the course of the business and the other as a private individual, of the implied warranties of fitness for purpose and merchantable quality laid down in the Sale of Goods Act 1979, while such exclusions and restrictions in other contracts of sale are subject to a test of reasonableness. In addition, sales of goods within the European Community are also subject to the no-fault liability provisions of the EEC Products Liability Directive, given force in the UK by the Consumer Protection Act 1987, which cannot be avoided by a contract term.

6.09   There are thus significant legal obstacles to the exclusion of liability, and even where it is possible, the test of reasonableness that it is necessary to satisfy will involve such questions as the relative bargaining powers of the parties, whether any inducement was offered to enter into the contract, and whether the existence and extent of the contractual term were sufficiently made known. An attempt, therefore, to exclude liability by contract cannot, therefore, be made in the certainty that it will be effective. An apparent transfer of liability may therefore turn out to be a form of inadvertent risk retention.

6.10   Even if the transfer of the financial consequences of liability is enforceable at law, and, whether it is done by means of an exclusion clause or by an indemnity clause which, while it does not shift the liability from one party to another, imposes an obligation on a party who would not otherwise be liable, to reimburse the costs involved, the transfer may still not achieve its object. The party to whom the consequences have been transferred may not be willing or able to meet the responsibilities undertaken. The transfer of risk is thus accompanied by the assumption of a credit risk. It is therefore common for indemnity clauses, at least, to be accompanied by a requirement to effect adequate insurance to cover the risks transferred, frequently in the joint names of the parties to the contract.

CHAPTER 7

RISK FINANCING

7.01   After the risk has been identified, measured and treated in the most appropriate manner, there will always, unless the risk has been avoided or eliminated, be a residual risk to be retained, and the question will arise of the best method of financing that residual risk. There are four options open:

1 — to pay for losses as they arise out of operating budgets, with no special financial provision being made;

2 — to set up an internal contingency fund to meet losses;

3 — to borrow to meet the cost of losses;

4 — to use the special form of risk transfer afforded by insurance.

7.02   **PAYING FOR LOSSES AS THEY ARISE**

This is the simplest method of risk financing, since it requires no special effort or administrative arrangements. It is, however, only suitable for a very restricted range of losses which have the following characteristics:

— low severity. Clearly, if the loss could reach serious proportions, there might not be sufficient funds to meet it.

— high predictability, which goes with frequent occurrence.

— a pattern of occurrence which matches the organisation's cash flow pattern. If, for example, it has a very seasonal business, while losses happen evenly through the year, there could be times when the funds to meet losses are not available, even though the losses are of a size which the organisation could meet without difficulty at other times in the year.

7.03   **ADVANTAGES**

This method or providing for losses does, however, have the following advantages:

— the money remains available to the organisation until it is needed to meet losses. Nothing has to be paid in advance as would be the case if the risk were insured.

— losses are paid net. No element of insurers' expenses has to be met. If small, frequent losses of this kind are insured, the premium calculation will inevitably come to mean that the insured will be called upon to meet the cost of claims plus the insurers' loading.

53

— there is some incentive to a minor degree of loss prevention since costs are included in a budget and abnormal levels of loss will have to be accounted for like any other budget variance.

7.04 DISADVANTAGES

— it is difficult to establish an effective reporting system for losses financed in this way, so that information which could indicate a change in the nature or size of the risk may not be available to the risk manager;

— credit is rarely given for underspending budgets, and there is therefore no incentive to reduce losses below the level included in the budget;

— this method tends to assume that each profit centre will meet its own losses from its budget. This reduces even more the size of loss that can be financed in this way, since without some form of centralisation or cross-subsidy between units of the organisation, retention has to be set at a level that can be borne by the smallest.

7.05 INTERNAL CONTINGENCY FUNDS

More serious losses may be financed by establishing a contingency fund, either by setting aside a sufficient capital sum, or by regular contributions, somewhat akin to internal insurance premiums, or by a combination of both. Such a fund can provide a means of spreading the cost of losses over a number of years since provisions not immediately used can be retained to meet future losses.

7.06 ADVANTAGES

— Funds are retained by the organisation and are available for investment until they are needed to pay claims;

— Claims are paid net, as with those financed from operating budgets;

— The size of contributions can be varied to reflect changes in cash flow; larger sums can be credited to the fund in good times, and contributions can be reduced when the financial situation is not so favourable. This flexibility is not available where financing is by insurance.

— The organisation has complete discretion to decide which losses shall be met from the fund.

7.07 DISADVANTAGES

— Contributions to an internal contingency fund, unlike insurance premiums, are not tax deductible;

— In the U.K., in common with most countries, it is not possible for companies other than insurance companies to make tax-free provisions for unidentified future losses. A fund cannot therefore be carried forward from one year to another without incurring a tax liability.

— There is always an opportunity cost involved in retaining funds within the organisation for purposes such as this when they could be used in more directly profit-oriented ways;

— Funds must be readily realisable to meet losses and therefore cannot be invested to obtain the maximum return;

— There is a danger that the fund may be diverted to other purposes within the organisation. It can be tempting to treat it as a reserve available to help the organisation in an adverse financial situation, or to divert some of it for general purposes if the loss record has been good and few claims have been made upon it. In either case, the fund may prove to be insufficient when a loss at the upper end of the range for which the fund was set up occurs.

— Large initial capitalisation may be necessary. If the fund is built up wholly out of contributions, the amount of loss that can be financed in the early years will have to be restricted or the fund may prove inadequate.

— stop loss protection to safeguard the fund against an unexpectedly large number of claims in a short period is very difficult to arrange.

7.08   POST-LOSS BORROWING

A further method of financing retained risk is to borrow funds as and when losses occur, either to meet all losses of a particular type, or to meet amounts which cannot be funded out of operating revenues.

7.09   ADVANTAGES

The main advantage of this method of funding is its flexibility. No action need be taken until the loss occurs, and the amount to be borrowed can be decided at that time on the basis of what is currently needed, rather than being set in advance on the basis of estimates.

7.10   DISADVANTAGES

The disadvantage of relying on credit as a means of funding losses is that one has no control over when the money will be needed and what the prevailing credit conditions will then be. If interest rates are high or credit is in short supply, the cost of funding loss in this way may be very high, and in extreme cases, the funds needed may not be available. In addition, the loss itself may have damaged or destroyed significant income-earning assets, and this will itself reduce the organisation's credit rating.

7.11   CONTINGENT LOANS

One possibility of ensuring that credit will be available is to arrange a contingent line of credit in advance. An agreement is entered into with a lender that a line of credit will be made available which can be drawn upon by the organisation when a loss occurs for which financing is needed. It may, however, be very difficult to find a lender ready to enter into such an arrangement and it will almost certainly prove to be an expensive method of borrowing. The lender has to ensure that funds to meet possible calls by the borrower are available at all times, and they cannot therefore be invested as profitably as might otherwise be the case. The interest rate for this type of arrangement is likely therefore to be high. A commitment fee will almost certainly be required in addition.

7.12 FACTORS INFLUENCING RISK RETENTION DECISIONS

Decisions on whether or not risks are to be retained, and the chosen method of financing those which are retained will be influenced by the following factors:

— **the degree of risk aversion of the organisation**. The greater the level of risk aversion, the less inclined the organisation will be to retain risk. The degree of risk aversion or preference will depend not only upon the individual approaches to risk of the key decision makers, but also upon the nature and objectives of the organisation. If it is a public company whose aims are essentially short-term and determined by the need to provide a good return to investors annually, risk retention will be more attractive than spending money upon avoiding, reducing or transferring risk. An organisation with longer-term aims, such as a family business, where continuance of the firm is the main objective, the tendency will be not to retain risks if other means of handling them are easily available. Similarly, a large organisation and one in a good financial position will have greater resources to enable it to retain more risk than a small one or one whose financial position is more precarious.

— **the nature and size of the risk**. Only risks which are of comparatively low severity, and of high predictability are normally suitable for retention. Furthermore, the pattern of losses must be compatible with the organisation's cash flow. If the organisation's business is essentially seasonal, there may be times of the year when even small losses cannot be met.

— **external incentives and disincentives**. The decision whether or not to retain risk and how to finance it may be influenced by factors outside the control of the organisation. The following are examples:

— compulsory insurance requirements may make the retention of some risks impossible;

— the availability and cost of credit will influence the use of loans to finance risk;

— taxation treatment of different financing methods may affect the choice between them. Thus the tax deductibility of insurance premiums may make insurance preferable to a contingency fund where contributions are not deductible;

— the availability of grants in areas where the government wishes to encourage development may reduce the replacement cost of some major assets to the extent that the severity of the risk of losing them becomes low enough for them to be retained.

CHAPTER 8

THE USE OF INSURANCE IN RISK MANAGEMENT

8.01   The conventional view of insurance is that of a fund which brings together the contributions (premiums) of many insureds, out of which the claims of the minority who suffer loss are met. The chief function of insurance is thus to replace uncertainty about the possibility of a major loss with the certain payment of a much smaller amount. This picture is true where individuals and small businesses are concerned, but for a large organisation approaching insurance as a risk management financing tool, and whose insurances may well be rated entirely upon its own record, the main value of insurance is as **a means of spreading the cost of losses over a sufficient number of years** for them to be borne.

8.02   This implies a recognition of the fact that the organisation will normally have to pay in premium, over the years, the cost of its own claims (other than those of catastrophic proportions, for which the catastrophe reserves and re-insurance arrangements of the insurer make up a pool of the type described above), plus the insurers' handling costs and profit, which becomes in effect a fee for the loss-spreading service. It follows from this that insurance, other things being equal, will be a financing method which is appropriate for risks which are too large to be borne in a single year, but which is likely to be too expensive for small risks. If the cost of losses can be met from an organisation's own resources without being spread over more than one year, there is little point in buying insurance if doing so increases the overall cost. The introduction of risk management within an organisation may thus lead to the cancellation of insurances of many small risks, and an increase of insurance cover where it is most valuable — against large and catastrophic risks.

8.03   It can be shown, in theory, that insurance would never be an economic proposition for a risk neutral person, who would not be prepared to pay more than a premium amounting to the probability of loss multiplied by the amount at risk, that is to say, the 'pure premium'. Since that pure premium will always have to be loaded by an amount to pay for the insurer's expenses and profit, insurance will always be too expensive for someone who is risk neutral. Nevertheless, insurance is a very important and very commonly used method of financing risk. The following are some of the reasons.

8.04   RISK AVERSION

Most organisations are not risk neutral, but tend to be to some extent risk averse where pure risks are concerned. They will therefore be prepared to pay more than the actuarially fair premium in order to have the security that insurance can provide.

8.05   ADDITIONAL SERVICES

The loading element of the premium charged includes the expense of providing some services, such as claims settlement or loss prevention advice, which are valued by the insured organisation or which it would have to provide for itself if the risk were uninsured. This may therefore provide an incentive to insure. In an extreme case, such as many engineering insurances, it may be the ancillary statutory inspection services which are the most important part of the purchase, with insurance cover as a subsidiary part of the package.

8.06   ADDITIONAL RISKS TRANSFERRED

By purchasing insurance, the insured not only transfers to the insurer the financial effects of the risk insured against, but also a number of associated risks:

— the **fluctuation risk**. Since the occurrence of pure losses is random, there is always the possibility that the loss experience may be very much higher than could have been predicted from the past record of the insured or of the industry of which it forms part. If the risk were retained, the organisation itself would have to find a means of financing this possibility, but if it insures, the risk falls upon the insurer.

— **investment risks**. If risks of any size are to be funded internally by the company, it will be necessary to invest funds to provide the resources necessary to meet the cost of losses. Fluctuations in the market may mean that returns on investments may not be as great as expected, so that reserves are inadequate. Maturity and liquidity of investment funds must be matched with the need for them. Since the occurrence of losses cannot be accurately predicted, this matching may not be achieved. This risk is also transferred to the insurer in return for the premium.

— **foreign exchange risks**. Where an organisation has operations in more than one country, provision for retained risks in countries other than the home country must include reserves in case of adverse changes in exchange rates between the countries concerned. This, too becomes the insurer's problem if the risks are insured.

8.07   COMPULSORY INSURANCES

In nearly, all countries some insurances are compulsory, and there is therefore no choice as to the risk financing method to be used. Each country has its own pattern of compulsory insurance, but motor and workers' compensation insurance are the most common compulsory classes, although liabilities for a wide range of specified activities, professional indemnities and even fire insurance may figure among compulsory classes.

8.08   TAXATION

In most countries, insurance premiums are normally deductible from corporation taxes. In all but a very few countries, it is not possible to make tax-deductible provisions for unknown losses, and contributions to internal contingency funds are therefore at a tax disadvantage compared with insurance premiums.

8.09   INSURANCE RATING METHODS

The conventional insurance rating method is that of **class rating**, by which the range of insureds is divided into groups according to the hazard each presents, a premium calculated for each class which is appropriate for the average insured in that class, and minor adjustments are then made according whether the individual insured is better or worse than the average for the class.

8.10   This system, which suits the individual or small commercial insured, and which derives from the model of insurance described in paragraph 8.01, is not particularly attractive to the larger insured wishing to make the best use of insurance in a risk management programme. The larger the organisation, the more its risks are likely to be unique, and thus unsuitable for aggregating with others in a risk class. The class rating system is also fairly inflexible, and the adjustments which can be made to class rates are often insufficient to give full recognition to a good record or well-developed loss control practices.

8.11   Use of insurance as a loss-spreading mechanism requires the premium for non-catastrophic losses to be based solely upon organisation's own record, i.e. by **experience rating**. Once it is accepted that insurance is a loss spreading and claims settling service, the premium becomes in effect a service fee, which lends itself to calculation by a formula based on the average claims cost over a period long enough to be representative without being so long as to make the past data irrelevant. To this will be added an amount as the contribution to a catastrophic claims fund which is contributed to by all the risks on the insurer's books.

8.12   PARTIAL INSURANCE

The most effective form of using insurance may not be to insure all levels of severity of a particular risk. It may be more appropriate to retain the risk of small losses, but to insure larger ones of the same kind. This can be achieved by means of a **deductible** or **franchise** of a suitable amount. Other possibilities are to retain a set proportion of each loss by means of **coinsurance**, or to insure up to the maximum level of foreseeable loss, and to retain the remote risk of a loss exceeding that amount, by means of a **first loss policy**.

8.13   Partial insurance may be attractive in the following circumstances:

- where there is a possibility of major loss, but most of the losses are likely to be small. A deductible or franchise gives protection against the loss which is too large to be retained, while not buying insurance protection unnecessarily for the small losses.

2) — where there is such a good spread of risk that a total loss is a near-impossibility, a first loss policy may be appropriate. The total loss by theft of the contents of a department store, for example, might be thought to be so improbable that a policy giving cover up to the maximum foreseeable loss might seem a more suitable use of insurance.

3) — Where a good-sized contingency fund can help to bear a proportion of each risk a coinsurance arrangement may be suitable, although some form of aggregate stop loss may be needed to protect the fund against too many losses occurring in a single year.

8.14 DISADVANTAGES OF PARTIAL INSURANCE

All partial insurance depends upon estimates of the probability and potential severity of losses. These estimates may always prove to be wrong, leaving the organisation retaining more risk than expected, which could expose it to losses it is ill-prepared to bear. Where the severity of loss has been under-estimated a first loss policy could prove to be an unfortunate choice, since it will be the upper end of the loss that is not covered; where frequency has been misjudged, coinsurance will prove more expensive than expected.

8.15 The premium reduction allowed for even a large deductible may not be as large as the risk manager considers to be justified in view of the extent of the risk being retained. It must, however, be remembered that the premium charged is made up of two elements:

— the pure premium for the risk;

— a loading to cover the insurer's expenses and profit.

Only the first of these varies proportionately with the risk, whereas the second may not be reduced to any great extent, except for the cost of handling small claims, by the existence of the deductible.

8.16 Where a large deductible is concerned, the effect is to retain the levels of loss which are most predictable, leaving the insurer with the larger losses where there is the greatest uncertainty both about frequency and severity. Since this involves both less predictability and a greater possibility of fluctuation in the results of insuring the risk, the insurer will require to retain some of the premium to contribute to a catastrophe reserve, which will diminish the amount available as a rebate for the deductible.

8.17 THE INSURANCE BUYING DECISION

Whether or not insurance is a suitable method of financing a specific risk will depend upon the answers to a number of questions:

— Does the cost of losses need to be spread over more than one year?

— Are the losses of too high an average cost and too unpredictable to be retained and funded internally?

— Is competition in the market such that sound insurers are offering covering at less than its true cost?

— Does the insurance premium also buy services which are necessary or desirable and which would be more expensive if purchased separately?

— Are the cover, conditions and limits available adequate to ensure that significant parts of the risk do not still have to be retained?

— Is the solvency of the proposed insurer and its reinsurers sufficiently proven?

— Is there a requirement to insure, either because insurance is compulsory by law, or required by the terms of a lease, debenture or other contract?

— What value does the organisation put upon being protected from risk and on paying a known cost?

CHAPTER 9

CAPTIVE INSURANCE COMPANIES

9.01 DEFINITION OF A CAPTIVE INSURANCE COMPANIES

A captive insurance company is an insurance company set up as the subsidiary of a company which is not itself an insurer, for the purpose of insuring or reinsuring some or all of its parent's risks. It may accept business from its parent and associated companies only, in which case it is called a **pure captive**. If it accepts business from other sources, it may be referred to as an **open market captive**. If it is formed jointly by two or more companies, who will normally be in the same industry, it is called a **multi-parent or association captive**. Where an insurance company provides an equivalent service by writing the risks of a single organisation in an entirely separate account, the arrangement is known as a **rent-a-captive**.

9.02 Captives are not a new phenomenon. In their modern form they represent an extension of the long-established practice of companies getting together to form a mutual insurance company to the case of a single company which has a sufficient spread of risk. Examples of single-owner captives have existed for many years, but it is only in the last quarter of a century that it has become the rule, rather than the exception, for any large company to number an insurance company among its subsidiaries, as part of its strategy for managing the risks that face it.

9.03 REASONS FOR FORMING A CAPTIVE

The trigger for the formation of many captives has been dissatisfaction with the services, methods or costs of the conventional insurance market. A captive has been seen as a way of overcoming one or more of the following problems:

— Inadequate recognition in the premium charged of a loss record or loss control standards substantially better than the average for the industry of which the organisation is part;

— Insufficient recognition by premium reduction of a substantial deductible;

— Inability to obtain cover for an unusual risk;

— Unacceptable restrictions or warranties contained in the policy;

— Inadequate maximum limits of cover.

9.04 ADVANTAGES OF FORMING A CAPTIVE

Use of a captive overcomes some of the disadvantages of an internal contingency fund. Among these is the difficulty commonly encountered in obtaining stop loss protection for a fund. It is one of the chief advantages of a captive that it gives an organisation **access to the reinsurance market**. It is the catastrophic end of the severity scale that is the risk manager's chief concern and reinsurers are specialists in catastrophe cover. Cover for that part of a risk which exceeds the organisation's own retention can therefore be obtained in a market which is cheaper, because its overheads are much lower than those of the direct market, where covers are much more closely experience-rated and credit is therefore given for a good loss record.

9.05   Unlike contributions to an internal fund, **premiums paid to a captive are tax deductible** in most countries, like those paid to any other insurance company, making a captive a more tax-efficient method of insuring. In the USA, however, the Internal Revenue Service has won a number of court decisions that premiums paid to a pure captive should not be tax deductible, on the grounds that such transactions, where the premiums and risk do not move outside a single economic grouping, do not involve the element of transfer of risk that is the distinguishing feature of insurance.

9.06   A captive provides a way of obtaining **insurance cover for risks which are uninsurable in the conventional market**. This advantage is, however, limited to the amount of an organisation's own retention, since if reinsurance is required, the captive is once more approaching the conventional market and reinsurers may be very reluctant to offer cover for a risk which departs too far from what is considered normal.

9.07   A captive, because it has the privileges of an insurance company in being able to carry loss reserves forward free of tax, is able to grow more quickly than an internal contingency fund, and so **increase the size of its parent's retention** of risk.

9.08   A captive can help a multinational organisation to establish a more uniform pattern of insurances around the world. In many countries, insurances of local risks must be placed with insurers who are authorised to write business locally. **Fronting arrangements** can often be made, whereby a local insurer writes the risk, thus complying with the local law, but then reinsures most of the risk with the captive, which then retrocedes the amount of the risk above its own retention with the reinsurance market in the normal way.

9.09   A domestic captive can become an approved insurer of **compulsory insurances**. Most captives are, however, established offshore, and cannot therefore be approved in this way, but they can still participate in the compulsory insurances of their parent by a fronting arrangement similar to that described in 9.08 above. Here, an approved insurer would insure the risk and comply with regulations such as those relating to the issue of insurance certificates, but would reinsure the bulk of the risk with the captive. Because fronting arrangements of one kind or another are so common, many captives are set up as reinsurance companies and not direct insurers.

9.10   Formation of a captive offers an **improvement in cash flow** for the organisation. Although premiums are paid to the captive, they do not pass outside the group, so that the organisation still has the use of the premiums retained by the captive until claims have to be paid. The captive will have to purchase reinsurance, but even here there is a benefit, as it is common for reinsurance premiums to be paid in instalments rather than in full in advance, as is usual for direct insurance premiums.

9.11   The advantages of a captive are increased where it is set up in an offshore tax haven. The reduced or non-existent taxation of underwriting profits and reserves mean that the captive can grow and retain a greater amount of risk more quickly. An offshore captive is not a tax avoidance device, since at best **tax is deferred** until funds are repatriated to the parent's home country as claims payments or profit.

9.12   The less stringent **authorisation and capitalisation requirements** of a tax haven make formation of the captive simpler and less expensive than would be the case in the organisation's home country and the necessary expertise in establishing and managing captives tend these days to be concentrated in such areas, because of their popularity as captive centres.

9.13   DISADVANTAGES OF A CAPTIVE

A captive is a long-term venture, which may not be particularly profitable in the early years. It must, however, be adequately capitalised, even though the level of capitalisation need not be as high as for a conventional insurance company, and this **capital will be tied up** and not available for other profitable ventures of the organisation.

9.14   The advantages of dealing in the **reinsurance market** have been outlined above, but there are also disadvantages. The credit given for a good record is balanced by an equally rapid penalty for a worsening experience, and it is essentially a market for professionals, who are expected to know what they are doing.

9.15   The tax authorities continue to mount an **attack on the tax advantages** of captives. The success of the IRS in opposing tax deductibility of premiums paid to pure captives in the USA has been mentioned in 9.05 above. In the UK, the Inland Revenue has concentrated on examining closely the management arrangements of offshore captives to make certain that the captive is in fact separate from its parent, is operated at arm's length and that underwriting decisions are taken in the captive location and not at the premises of the parent. In addition, a UK parent must be aware of the "controlled foreign company" provisions of the Finance Act 1984, which treat a subsidiary established in a tax haven of a UK-domiciled company as being subject to UK taxation unless it can bring itself within one of a number of exemptions. As far as a captive insurance company is concerned, the significant qualifications are the following:

— the "motive test". Here it would have to be shown that tax advantage was not a main motive in establishing the captive in a low tax area. Clearly, this would in most cases be a very difficult test to meet.

— the "exempt activities test". This is met if the company derives more than 50 per cent of its income from sources other than its parent group. This test cannot be met by a pure captive, but can be satisfied by an open market, multi-parent or association captive.

— the "acceptable distribution test". Provided at least 50 per cent of profits are remitted each year, UK taxation will not be levied on the balance. This is the test which will be applicable to most pure captives. It reduces the ability of the captive to grow quickly, but does not eliminate it, and the balance of convenience and advantage still leads most captives to be formed offshore.

9.16 A captive will involve the commitment of **management time**, particularly in the early stages. The advantage to the organisation must therefore be sufficient and the captive a sufficiently significant part of the organisation's risk financing strategy to make it worth while.

9.17 There are specific **disadvantages of multi-parent captives**.

— Since these are normally formed by companies which are in the same industry, there is always a possibility that all may be affected by the same disaster.

— if the loss records of the various partners differ widely, it may be difficult to find an acceptable form of **rating** which does not involve a subsidy from the organisation with the better record.

— if one party wishes to withdraw from the captive, there may be insufficient spread of risk among the remaining parties to make some risks suitable for the captive, which may thus cease to be viable. Suitable **withdrawal** procedures must therefore be agreed at the outset.

9.18 **PREREQUISITES FOR A SUCCESSFUL CAPTIVE**

To operate a successful captive, an organisation must:

— treat it as a long-term venture which is part of an overall plan for the financing of risk;

— have an adequate spread of risk to enable the captive's retentions to be large enough to justify its existence;

- have an adequate system of risk identification and measurement;
- maintain an effective loss control programme;
- have full records of past loss experience, so that the best possible predictions may be made of future losses.
- carry out a full feasibility study before establishing the captive.

9.19 FEASIBILITY STUDIES

The purpose of a captive feasibility study is to ensure that a captive is only set up if it can be justified as a reasonable part of an organisation's risk financing programme, and to ensure that the right choices are made about the form, location and management of the captive, the nature and extent of the risks to be written and the reinsurance programme. It can be carried out internally, but as few organisations will have staff with all the necessary knowledge and experience of captives, it is common for the study to be carried out by an external consultant.

9.20 The feasibility study should begin with an assessment of the reasons why a captive is being suggested, the problems it is designed to solve, or the particular advantage it is hoped it will bring, so that the basic questions on which all the remainder of the study hang can be answered. That question is whether a captive is an appropriate way of achieving the organisation's aims, and whether the chances of success are such that the investment in time and money which it represents will be justified.

9.21 If the proposal meets this test, then the study must examine the needs of the organisation and design a captive to meet those needs. This will include consideration of the following:

- the location of the captive: is it to be a domestic or an offshore captive? If the latter, which captive centre is the most suitable?
- Is it to be established as a direct insurance company or as a reinsurance captive?
- what level of capitalisation is desirable;
- potential premiums available to the captive: are they sufficient to make it viable?
- which classes of insurance are most suitable for the captive?
- what is to be the underwriting policy of the captive? What rating techniques will it use?
- how much risk will the captive be able to retain? What is the most appropriate reinsurance programme for amounts above the retention?

— how is the captive to be managed? Will the organisation itself run it, or is a captive management company to be used? If so, what services will it be expected to supply, and can the administrative requirements be met in the preferred location? How will the managers be selected?

— who will manage the investment of the captive's funds?

— will any claims settlement or other specialist services be required?

9.22 The feasibility study therefore amounts to an examination of the justification for a captive and the construction of a business plan for it, so that its viability can be tested before the organisation becomes committed to its formation. It is an essential step, because a captive formed for the wrong reasons, or without the necessary top management backing, or in the wrong place or writing the wrong risks will be unlikely to contribute as constructively as it should to the overall risk financing programme and may well be no more than an expensive toy.

CHAPTER 10

THE ORGANISATION OF RISK MANAGEMENT

10.01 THE ROLE OF THE RISK MANAGER

The risk manager's role will vary from one organisation to another, and there is no generally-accepted pattern of functions which all risk managers will fulfil. The view of risk management which sees the risk manager as being responsible for identifying, measuring, treating and financing all the risks of an organisation is, however, rarely advanced seriously these days, as it is apparent that no one person can have all the technical knowledge, the skills or even the time to carry out such a brief. Since risk affects everything an organisation does or has done to it, such a risk manager would have effectively to run the entire organisation.

10.02 The first limitation on the risk manager's role that is seen in most organisations is that the risk manager has little involvement with speculative risks. There is no reason in theory why this should be so, since the principles of managing financial and other business risks are exactly the same as those involved in the management of pure risks, but virtually all organisations find it convenient for operational purposes that pure and speculative risks should be handled by different persons.

10.03 It is unlikely in practice that the risk manager will have sole or even the primary responsibility for the management of all pure risks. Many of the major risks that face the organisation will be closely connected with the production, marketing, distribution or other factors, and the major responsibility for managing the risks will rest with the line manager responsible for the function in question. Good risk management can often not be separated from good operating practice and it would be unwise to try to divide responsibility for achieving it between two managers.

10.04 The risk manager's role is therefore more likely to be advisory, with the following three aspects to it:

- co-ordinator;
- educator;
- activator.

10.05 CO-ORDINATION

Risk management is most successful in a company if everyone participates in it. There is a need, however, for someone at the centre to co-ordinate the activities of the various line managers

— to ensure that a **common policy** is being followed, so that the risk management efforts of one department do not adversely affect the risk pattern of another;

— to ensure that the programme being adopted is one which fits the organisation's **corporate objectives**, and its attitude to risk and its individual management style.

— to ensure that there are no **gaps between areas of responsibility** which could enable serious risks to remain unidentified. The risk manager may often assume responsibility for managing such risks if they are not more appropriately the responsibility of another manager.

— to collate the **regular reports** on risk, its effects and treatment which will form an important part of the administration of most risk management programmes.

10.06 In a highly-decentralised organisation, it may well be necessary for one manager at each operating unit to act as a local risk management co-ordinator, with the central risk manager in turn co-ordinating their efforts.

10.07 EDUCATION

It is not sufficient that risk management should become part of the responsibilities of each line manager; each must be made aware of its importance and of how his activities affect the management of other risks faced by the organisation. This educational function is one that the risk manager will usually have to carry out. It will involve drafting and drawing attention to the organisation's risk management policy statement, which is usually issued over the signature of top management and establishes both the importance and the status of risk management within the organisation. This may in turn form part of a full risk management manual in organisations where management instructions are normally embodied in manuals. In addition the risk manager must use the visits he carries out to the various units of the organisation to introduce everyone to the concept and practice of risk management, so that it becomes an integral part of the way the operation is managed.

10.08 THE ROLE AS ACTIVATOR

This part of the risk manager's role is closely connected with the role as activator. It is not sufficient that there should be a good awareness of risk and the methods of managing it in the organisation. There must also be a positive approach to risk management, and it will be part of the function of the risk manager to encourage this in every possible way.

10.09 LINE MANAGEMENT RESPONSIBILITIES

The risk manager's role may be essentially advisory, but most risk managers in practice are directly responsible for implementing certain aspects of the risk management programme. Since the majority of risk managers come from an insurance background, they frequently have direct responsibility for arranging insurance of those risks which are to be financed in this way. This is by no means an essential part of the risk manager's own role, however; it is largely a consequence of the development of the function, and it would be equally possible for there to be an insurance expert who reported to the risk manager, or for the risk manager to have particular responsibility for another function, such as safety, security or fire prevention, about which his earlier training had given him expert knowledge.

10.10 THE RISK MANAGER'S PLACE IN THE ORGANISATIONAL STRUCTURE

Because most risk management departments have developed from insurance departments, it is common for a risk manager to report either to a financial executive or to the company secretary, as these are the most common reporting lines for insurance management. One cannot, however, be dogmatic about what is the correct place for the risk manager to occupy in the organisational structure. Every organisation will be different, and the place of risk management in the structure, like any other aspect of risk management, must be designed to fit in with the particular style and needs of the particular organisation. One can, however, set out some features which are desirable for the risk manager's reporting line. It must combine:

— access to top management;

— sufficient authority to enforce necessary change;

— a position where it is easy to be informed about all aspects of the organisation's activities;

— a good communications network;

— independence of sectional interests in the organisation.

10.11 REPORTING TO A FINANCIAL EXECUTIVE

This is the reporting line which is suitable for most organisations. It provides access to a senior member of the management team, whose responsibilities embrace every that the organisation does or plans to do. It should ensure that risk management becomes a fully-integrated part of the organisation's financial management, and is particularly appropriate since the effects of risk are felt by the organisation in financial terms, and risk management can therefore be reasonably considered a financial discipline. This reporting line also offers the best opportunity for close integration of the management of pure and speculative risks. The disadvantages may be too rigid a cost-benefit approach to risk management projects, for many of which both costs and benefits, particularly the indirect ones, may be very difficult to quantify, possible remoteness, both geographically and operationally, from some of the major production units, where the risk manager will need to have close contacts, and possible resentment from those units if the risk manager appears to be able to obtain funds for risk management projects in preference to their competing proposals because of his closeness to the finance director.

10.12 REPORTING TO A COMPANY SECRETARY

This reporting line again offers the necessary central position in the organisation, and close access to top management, since the company secretary serves the board, if not a member of it. It is a neutral department which is not closely identified with any of the major operating functions, and subsidiaries and divisions of the organisation will usually have their own secretarial departments which will in the normal course of business be in regular close communication with the group secretariat, and can thus often provide the risk manager with a ready-made network through which information about risk and changes in it can readily be received. The disadvantages may include too great an emphasis on insurance as a risk management solution, a possible tendency towards bureaucracy and a remoteness similar to that mentioned in connection with reporting to a financial executive. This is, however, often a very suitable reporting line in organisations where risks are largely controllable by organisational rather than by technical means, or in a very diversified company which has a highly decentralised management style. In such an organisation, administrators, such as the company secretary, often have better links with all parts of the organisation than any others in the organisation, and this can be of very great help to the risk manager.

10.13 REPORTING TO THE CHIEF EXECUTIVE

A direct reporting line to the chief executive obviously meets the needs of central location and access to authority better than any other and no position for the risk manager could more clearly indicate the importance an organisation puts upon risk management. There are, however, many drawbacks. The apex of the management pyramid can be remote from the areas most immediately affected by risk, and there can be a conflict between the needs of risk management, which is very often a matter of detail, and the broad policy decisions which are the normal concern of the chief executive. The demands upon the chief executive's time may make it difficult for the risk manager to keep in close enough touch with the person to whom he reports, particularly if the chief executive travels extensively. There can also be difficulties for the risk manager, who will frequently have to ask many questions about the organisation's operations. A risk manager is too closely identified with the chief executive may easily be seen as a spy for top management and not receive the co-operation which is essential for risk management to become successful. This reporting line can, however, be successful in a small or very compact one, or in a very decentralised company, where the risk manager forms part of a small administrative group, and the emphasis is firmly on the co-ordinating aspects of the job.

10.14 REPORTING TO A TECHNICAL DIRECTOR

This may be a suitable reporting line in a science-based organisation, where a proper understanding of the major risks calls for a scientific or technical background, and where those risks are primarily controlled by technical means. The drawback, as with any reporting line which means that the risk manager, whose interests must include a very wide range of risks facing the organisation, reports to a specialist in risks of a particular kind, is that too much emphasis will be placed on risks with a technical solution and simpler, non-technical risks may in consequence tend to be under-managed.

10.15 OTHER REPORTING LINES

There are many other possible reporting lines which may be suitable in particular cases. Among these are reporting to:

— an **administrative director** or **group services director**

This reporting line is one which recognises the fact that the risk manager offers a service to the whole organisation, and which provides the necessary access to a central authority. The main drawback can be that risk management may be one of a number of very diverse activities for which this director is responsible. It is very difficult for anyone to give equal attention to all of them in such a case, especially when, as is often the case, the director is a specialist who has been promoted by having additional responsibilities added to his main area of expertise. There will be a strong tendency to devote more attention to the director's main area of interest than to the others, and risk management may suffer if it is one of the additional responsibilities.

— a **legal director**. This reporting line is more common in continental Europe than it is in the United Kingdom. It could be appropriate in an organisation where liability risks predominate, particularly if the organisation is not a manufacturing concern.

— a **property director** or **estates director**. This might be suitable where the organisation's risks are centred around the large number of properties it owns.

10.16 The above list does not exhaust the possibilities. Wherever an organisation is faced with major risks of a specialist nature, it will often be appropriate for the risk management function to be part of a department which has a special concern with those risks. The risk manager may be located anywhere in the organisation that enables him to be aware of risk and changes in it quickly, enables him to co-ordinate efforts to deal with it and to encourage, and if necessary enforce changes to improve risk management.

TABLE OF STATUTES

INDEX

Risk pattern 2.12, 5.03
Risk perception 3.01
Risk preference 1.04, 7.12
Risk reduction, loss control and loss prevention 2.07, 5.05–5.42, 7.03, 8.05, 9.03, 9.18
Risk retention 2.09, 7.01–7.12, 8.17, 9.07
Risk transfer 2.08, 6.01–6.10
Risk treatment 2.05–2.11

S

Safety 5.09, 5.16–5.20, 10.09
Safety audits 3.16–3.17
Safety publications 3.04
Sale of Goods Act 1979 6.08
Security 5.09, 5.21–5.25, 10.09
Severity, measurement of 2.04, 4.01, 4.10–4.29, 8.14
Site plans 3.04
Site visits 3.03, 3.20
Social costs 2.17
Solvency of insurers 8.17
Speculative risks 1.05, 5.04, 10.02, 10.11
Spreading cost of loss 7.05, 8.01–8.02, 8.11, 8.17

Spread of risk 2.09, 8.13, 9.18
Standard conditions 3.04
Static risks 1.06
Stop loss 7.07, 8.13, 9.04
Subjective risk 1.04

T

Taxation 7.07, 7.12, 8.08, 9.05, 9.15
Technical directors 10.14
Threats 3.06, 3.11
Trade journals 3.04
Trivial risks 4.11

U

Uncertainty 1.02–1.03
Undesired consequences 1.02, 3.08, 3.12
Unfair Contract Terms Act 1977 6.06–6.08
Uninsurable risks 9.03, 9.06

W

Work in progress 4.16
Worker's compensation insurance 8.07